YOUNG IMAGINATION

Writing and artwork by children of New South Wales

edited by Susan Roy and Jeremy Steele

I love to imagine things because it's fun —
like I'm imagining that I'm the sea and the
waves and people swim in me or I'm a book
and people write in me.

Jenny McLean (7) Woy Woy South PS

PRIMARY ENGLISH TEACHING ASSOCIATION

This publication was partially funded by the New South Wales
Bicentennial Council to celebrate Australia's Bicentenary in 1988.

ISBN 0 909955 79 4
Dewey 808.89'9282
First published February 1988
Revised impression printed August 1989 for Heinemann Educational Books
70 Court Street Portsmouth New Hampshire 03801
Copyright this collection © Primary English Teaching Association 1988
PO Box 167 Rozelle NSW 2039
Copyright in all material is retained by individual contributors
Requests to reproduce original material should be addressed to the publishers
Project co-ordinator: Susan Roy
Production editor: Jeremy Steele
Design consultant: Mark Jackson
Typeset in 12/14 Times by Cider Press
11 Edward Street Balmain NSW 2041
Printed by Bridge Printery
29-35 Dunning Avenue Rosebery NSW 2018

CONTENTS

Bodies 1

Perceptions 5

Homes 10

Families 11

Schools 17

Happenings 20

Outdoors 23

Friends 26

Pets 30

Animal Stories 34

Nature 38

Rain 43

Fire 45

Australian Images 48

Fun 53

Tall Tales 57

In Space 63

Magic 66

Ghosts 69

Witches 72

Fairies 75

Two Poems 77

Short Stories 79

Longer Stories 90

PREFACE

Early in 1986 the NSW Bicentennial Council invited PETA to publish a book of writing and illustrations by children from NSW primary schools, to be part-funded by the Council. The PETA Board welcomed this proposal enthusiastically, and a sub-committee comprising Jean Koshemakin, Robyn Platt and Lyn Wilkie was formed. A co-ordinator, Susan Roy, was appointed in November.

The first notification of the project was sent out to schools in February/March 1987 and about 650 requested further information. Comment from many schools suggests that a great deal of interest was generated, and perhaps the most valuable feature of the project at this stage was the amount of discussion that went on at all levels within the schools.

By the beginning of Term 3 more than 3500 pieces of writing had been sent in to PETA by a wide range of schools throughout NSW — a range which the published pieces reflect. Submissions of artwork were relatively few by comparison.

It was never envisaged that the book should attempt to represent merely an average level of achievement at any particular age, and reading and re-reading the entries reinforced our belief that we should look for work distinguished by some kind of excellence. Judgements about quality will always vary, but we have consulted closely about ours and believe that the richness and variety on the pages which follow will reward most readers, even if they themselves might have made a slightly different selection.

We do regret that some beautifully illustrated work was executed on a scale that precluded reproduction. Similarly we regret that with some of the longer stories we have had to be content with quite short extracts: they are good enough to print in their entirety.

The presentation of material sent in to PETA varied considerably. Some pieces were in the author's handwriting, some in the teacher's and many more were typewritten. Most had clearly been edited. We decided that since most spelling had already been standardised, it would be distracting and misleading to retain any non-standard forms (which were not necessarily the author's anyway).

There is much more room for personal choice in punctuation style than in spelling, whatever a writer's age. We have chosen to follow the punctuation style of each piece as closely as possible, with some concessions to internal consistency (e.g. with the punctuation of direct speech). Otherwise alterations have only been made when sense or clarity seemed to demand them, which was seldom, and idiosyncratic styles have been preserved. Our policy over paragraph divisions has been the same, though we have occasionally had to run two paragraphs together (or drop a title) to gain space.

Almost all the pieces are printed complete, and we have included as many line illustrations as possible. In a very few cases the first paragraph or two of a piece has been omitted and this is signalled by three dots at the beginning. When we have only been able to include extracts from longer pieces, the word 'From' appears beside the title, and again any omissions are signalled by dots. All titles are the authors'.

We should make it clear that the sections into which the book is divided did not form part of the guidelines sent out to schools, but emerged during the selection process.

Finally, we should like to thank all the children and teachers who took part in the Young Imagination project. We hope they will find that the book which has grown out of their talents and enthusiasm is a satisfying reward for all their work.

Susan Roy & Jeremy Steele
Birchgrove, January 1988

BODIES

There are all types of bodies except it's only the skin that is different, but inside it is the same. We sometimes have the same hair and we have got the same ears and mouth, but we don't have the same eyes.

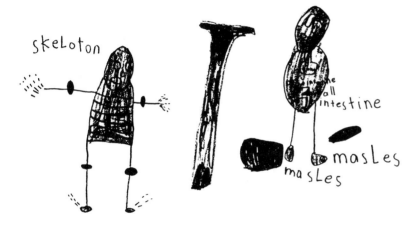

Adam Perry (6) Matthew Pearce PS, Baulkham Hills

❧ BONES ❧

Your Bones are very important to you. If you didn't have them you would just flop. Rag dolls don't have any bones and look how they flop. If you break a bone it hurts a lot and you have to keep it still for a long time. When you take all your skin and flesh off it would leave a skeleton. There are so many bones in your body. There are two hundred and six. There are joints in your body too and they help you bend. If you didn't have them you would just have to stand stiff. There is another part of your body called cartilage but it's soft bone. If you feel the end of your nose it's soft because it's cartilage too. Bones help you in so many ways. If I were you I would look after your Bones (and cartilage too).

Ben Shaw (7) Balgowlah Heights PS

❧ MY FACE ❧

My face is smooth and soft. My dad's face has whiskers. His face is rough and bumpy. My mother's face is smooth too. My dog Fluffy has fur on his face but he growls when you touch it. My family likes my face. I like my face too. My face is sticky when I eat lollies. Lollies are sticky.

Nicole Tromans (6) Rutherford PS

🐦 MY FIRST LOOSE TOOTH 🐦

My first loose tooth was the one on the left side. Dad said to me, do you want me to get a bit of string and tie it to the door handle? I'll get someone to slam the door and your tooth will come out. I said, NO WAY!

Elizabeth McKenna (6) Coonabarabran PS

🐦 HANDY HANDS 🐦

Leigh's got red hands
I've got blue.
My hands are padded and
Yours are too.
My hands are lumpy
Your hands are bumpy
I like hands
Do you like them too?

Leah Radford (9) John Warby PS, Airds

🐦 WHEN I WENT TO THE SCHOOL DOCTOR 🐦

One day at school, I went to the school doctor. We came into a big white room, and the nurse told us to sit down. One by one we went to have a needle. When it was my turn, I closed my eyes tightly, so as not to feel the pain. I was surprised to think it didn't hurt, but even if it didn't hurt at all, the nurse gave me a bandage. After we had all had our needle, we had to have our ear, mouth, and heart checked. I had a great day.

Rachel Axsentieff (8) Bankstown West PS

🐦 MY LIFE AS A DIABETIC 🐦

When I was 14 months old I got a throat infection and I turned into a diabetic. That means I am not allowed to eat sugar but I am allowed to eat cheese and meats.

If I get low I have to have some sugar quickly or I will have an attack.

I can't run around too much or that is when I can have an attack. But I can run around a little bit. I can be active.

Even though I am a diabetic I still am very good at things. I am a pretty good worker. I can do everything that other people can do.

I like being a diabetic because you don't get fat at all, and if I lose weight I have to eat some carbohydrates.

Andrew Weir (7) Plattsburg PS, Wallsend

❧ HOW IT FEELS BEING ON KIDNEY DIALYSIS ❧

I chose to interview my father and family on what they feel about my father being on the Kidney Machine because I wanted to share my family's feelings with you.

My name is Laurette Kairouz, I have a father whose name is Bernard Kairouz. My father is on a Kidney Machine. My father has been on Kidney Dialysis for a long 11 years. My mother Salma assists my father to the Kidney Machine, and has said it is very scary in case she makes a mistake.

When my father is taken off the Machine, he feels very dizzy, tired and sleepy.

When my father goes to hospital for a kidney transplant, and it doesn't work, he feels very sad and says to himself, "Why did this have to happen to me?"

I also asked my brothers and sister if anyone teased them at school about my father, they said no one did.

I'd like to ask all of you if you can pray for my father, that his next operation for his kidneys will be a successful operation and that he does not have to wait long for a donor.

How the Kidney Dialysis helps my Father

When my father wakes up at 5 o'clock in the morning, he is very tired. He puts the needles into his arms himself. When I touched the lumps on my father's arm, I always feel a sort of buzzing. When he has put the needles in his arm, he calls my mum, and my mum finishes putting him on the Kidney Machine. When the tubes are all connected he is ready to be on the Kidney Machine. He sleeps on a bed for 6 hours and the blood runs through the tubes and the Machine cleans the blood before it goes back into his body.

Thank You.

Laurette Kairouz (10) St Joseph's, Belmore

❧ From JOHN WOODEN'S HOSPITAL DIARY ❧

5/2/87
Recess: I thought I was shot in the stomach.
Lunch: It hurt to walk.
P.E: I was pale and I thought I was going to throw up – missed P.E.
Hometime: I was walking very slowly. I had a headache. I thought I was going to die! I thought to myself, "I probably just have to go to the toilet." So I went to the toilet. It didn't help. When I got home I had a Disprin with orange juice to take away my headache. Then I groaned all the way into bed. My Mum said, "What is wrong?" So I said, "I have a headache and I think I'm going to die!" She said, "Mmmm, it could be appendicitis." Then Mum said to Dad, "Do you think I should take him down to casualty?" Dad said, "Okay."

So we went up to Camperdown Children's Hospital and we were told to go to the X-ray Department to get some X-rays.

When we got there a lady told me to take off my shirt and to stand up straight in front of the machine. After two X-rays we went back and a doctor was squeezing my stomach when he said, "Go and wait in the hall for about three hours and keep him nil by mouth." So we went up the hall. Mum was sitting up and I went to sleep on her lap for three hours.

Then we were told to go inside a room full of beds. A nurse put a tight belt on my arm to make the veins stick up. Some blood was taken from my arm for pathology. Then a beautiful nurse put a long needle into the back of my hand, it had a tiny container on the back of it! Another needle was put into the tiny container to stop the blood from clotting. Then the nurse took the lid off the tiny container and connected a drip onto it. The nurse said, "You're a strange boy, when the needles are being put in, you smile!" Then she put tape all over my arm, then they stuck a foam stick under my arm to keep my arm straight and they put a half a coffee cup on my needle to protect the drip in my main vein. Then I was put onto a bed that was pushed into the ward. On the bedhead it said "NIL BY MOUTH. John Wooden 44 7819 23/09/76 Clubbe Ward 10.5 years Dr Martin." . . .

6/2/87

The next morning at 6.00 a.m. all the patients were woken up, all except for me because I fell asleep at 1.00 a.m!

At 8.00 a.m. the nurse woke me up and said, "I will be taking care of you all the time you are here." Then I thought to myself, "Gee I am lucky, blonde, tall, slim, nice, gentle and best of all, PRETTY! Wow!" Then she bathed me! I thought to myself, "This is going too far!" Then she put me onto a chair and made my bed. She then put me back on the bed where I stayed all day! At 5.00 p.m. the nurse came and pricked my finger. Then she squeezed two bottles of blood to be tested. At 6.00 p.m. the nurse put a needle in my bottom. 15 minutes later my eyes were going up and down! So I asked the nurse why my eyes were going up and down. She said, "It's just the needle making you drowsy, just close your eyes." Then a man put me onto another bed. I was pushed down to the operating theatre. I was still awake, just, when Dr Martin put a mask over my face. Then he put a needle in my drip. The next second I was unconscious!

7/2/87

At 6.00 a.m. I woke up. My stomach was hurting even more! So I looked at my stomach, I saw a cut with blood and a plastic covering over it! Then I looked at my hand, the name tag was missing! I then asked the nurse, "Why is my name tag missing?" The nurse said, "I took it off in recovery because you wouldn't wake up, I thought you were dead, and also because we couldn't feel your pulse." Then I said, "Then why wouldn't I wake up?" The nurse then said, "You wouldn't wake up because you fainted during the operation!" . . .

8/2/87

. . . At 6 p.m. the medicine man came around and said, "How many drugs are you on?" I said, "Three." He said, "What kind?" Since I didn't need any medicine I said, "Heroin, marijuana and cocaine!" All the nurses laughed and the man blushed. Then he said, "Very funny!". . .

17/2/87

I came back to the hospital to have the plastic on my cut taken off. When I said hello to the nurse she said, "Come back on April Fool's Day to have a check up."

John Wooden (10) Concord PS

PERCEPTIONS

❧ SMILING ❧

I like smiling at sad people.
They are poor. They always be sad.
Give them a big smile.

Sonya Restagno (6) Griffith East PS

❧ TODAY: YESTERDAY'S TOMORROW AND ❧ TOMORROW'S YESTERDAY

Yesterday, today, the future,
But the future never comes,
For the future becomes the present,
Only for a fleeting moment,
Then,
Only then,
Future becomes past,
The past forever.

❧ TIME AND LIFE ❧

The present is literally nothing,
But it is reality,
Reality for nothing but a split second,
Then it becomes the past.

The past affects the present through memories,
Memories of reality,
But the present present doesn't affect the past!
Rather the present present affects the future,
It affects the future through hopes in imagination,
Imagination of reality to come.

So the three components of time,
Past, present and future correlate in life.

Jonathan Wilson Fuller (7) Correspondence School

❧ WOW! I CAN DO IT NOW! ❧

When I was a toddler I wanted to play with my old dog, but he was tied up. I wanted to go and walk with my mum to get my brother, but I couldn't because I had to sit in my pram.

I could not sleep in a bed. I had to sleep in a cot.

I wanted to drink out of a glass, but I had to drink out of my bottle. I wanted to ride a bike, but I was too small.

Now, I can do everything.

Gizelle Kiss (7) OLQP, Greystanes

❧ THE OLD MAN ❧

Withered as a dry leaf
Decrepit and old
Bent and battered by time past
Frightened by the cold.

A very gnarled old tree
Once so straight and tall
Not knowing what the future holds
Waiting for the fall.

Katherine Ters (11) Wenona, North Sydney

❧ I AM A JUNK YARD ❧

I am a junk yard
no good anymore
I am rubbish on a dirt floor
I am scrap metal
old and torn

I am smelly air
I am rotting wood
on an old wooden bench
I am a rusty thing ragged and poor
I am a tyre worn out
I am a junk yard
no good anymore

Angus Turner-Robertson (10) Mosman C of E Prep

Why do some people do things wrong? Because they don't think and that means they have no brains. The people that have got a brain are lucky because they CAN think. I have got a brain. How about you?

Peter Baksheev (6) Tuggerawong PS

6

When I grow up I want to be a millionaire. I could buy a Porsche and a Suzuki and maybe even a ship, my own house, a milk bar, everything a millionaire would want. When I grow old I'll sell everything except my house because I'm weak and not strong enough now to look after it. When I die I'll go up to live with God in peace, beautiful sunshine, lovely birds. Our pets will be free and everybody's pets will be there. That's how I would like it to be. No sin in heaven; all will be good, no fighting, no guns, no weapons in heaven. God didn't make weapons in his country. No way. So that is how I would like it to be. How about you? How would you like it to be?

Jeffery Ottaway (8) Epping Heights PS

❧ LEAVE US ALONE ❧

Leave us alone; we're the same you see,
You're an animal just like me.
How would you like getting killed all across the land
And then be put in packets or even canned?
How would you like your guts taken out by a kangaroo,
And then be made into human bean stew?

What about the Tasmanian Tiger?
It was here one year,
And then all men caused it to disappear.

It's like the Aborigines;
You took away their land.
And I won't be surprised
If they're packeted and
CANNED.

Paul Kildea (9) McAuley PS, Rose Bay

❧ DUCK HUNTING ❧

The duck season has just opened. Duck hunters say that they should be able to shoot because it is just like any other sport. They say that they only shoot for food and don't shoot any endangered species.

The conservation and animal liberation groups think differently. They say that many protected ducks are being shot. They also think that some of the ducks have been shot and left to die a cruel death. A recent search proved this to be true. Several ducks were found alive but suffering from critical wounds.

Duck shooters have been heard as early as 6 a.m. and as late as 7 p.m., meaning that duck shooters could hit anything in the dark. A duck shooter recently drowned while trying to retrieve a duck from a deep lake.

Alain Hosking (10) Lane Cove West PS

❧ ONCE THERE WAS . . . ❧

Once there was fresh air,
now there is pollution.
Once there were trees,
now there are stumps.
Once there were clear rivers,
now they are polluted.
Once there were sacred places,
now they are public.
Once there was no violence,
now there are wars.
Once there was a land of beauty
but where has it gone?

Amanda Jessup (10) Holy Family, Lindfield

❧ POLLUTION ❧

Pollution is awful, especially in lakes where fish swim. I don't like it one bit because nearly everywhere I go there is rubbish and I pick it up.

Sara Sherwood (6) Bellambi PS

❧ THE APPLE CORE ❧

A long time ago two apple-seed-like things floated in outer space and landed on a planet called Earth.

Out of these "apple seeds" formed two armies called Nebulie and Fronshore. These two armies were always dressed in red and their blood was black as ink.

They had no minds of their own; only their commander gave the orders. No-one wanted to be in the army but they were not sad or unhappy because their commander said that they weren't.

One day the Nebulie commander decided they would have a war.

The Fronshore commander said, "I want the world to spin around in the West direction."

But then the Nebulie commander shouted, "I want it to go to the East and whatever I say goes."

The Fronshore commander yelled, "Forward!" and so did the Nebulie commander. Both armies began to fight.

They tore the soft soil with their guns, and bombs shook the ground and caved in the rivers and creeks.

Machine guns made the trees fall, and the commander just said, "It's only a silly tree," or "It's only a small creek," or "The soil is not so precious."

Every time the guns or bombs landed on earth, a handful of dirt floated off into space.

"Pow Pow," now the Earth was only about as big as an elephant.

"Pow Pow," the ground was black from the blood that they shed.

"Pow Pow," the Earth was now as big as an apple core but the armies kept fighting.

Now no-one was left on Earth, it was empty and grey. The apple core let out its first seeds which floated in outer space and landed on a planet called Neptune.

Out of these "apple seeds" formed two armies called Nebu-lie and Fronshore . . .

Celeste Lazarenko (10) Birchgrove PS

❧ DEADLY SECRETS ❧

There once was a man,
Simple man,
Deadly man.
He knew all secrets,
Simple secrets,
Deadly secrets.
He had control with a red button,
Simple button,
Deadly button.
And that man had all he wanted,
Simple things,
Deadly things.
He controlled all the world with a red button,
Simple button,
Deadly button.

Nathan Ollerenshaw (12) Leeton PS

❧ THE WORLD ❧

When innocent children view the world
It's a place of paradise.
With a special touch of beauty and happiness
With kind loving parents
With all their needs at hand.

The clear sparkling of the morning dew
The freshness of the windy air
The myriad colours of the rainbow.
They see themselves
Holding hands and playing happily
Oh! Life is so wonderful!

As time speeds on, books and schools
Help them understand
The depths of the horrible world –
The kindness of their own world lost
The fighting and killing of one another
For riches and lands.
The greediness of some people
Exploiting nature and everything on Earth.
But what do they gain
In the last minute of their life?
Nothing. Nothing at all –
No riches, no wealth, no land,
Nothing but regrets.
Then perish in remorse.

Why won't people hold hands
And live peacefully?
That dream is worth fulfilling.
In the short span of our lives
We should find ways to live together
Not excuses for living apart.

So, when you are rewarded
Ask for nothing else, nothing else at all
But to be at peace.

Thi Dao Tran (12) Bankstown West PS

HOMES

When I went to my house it had eyes and a nose and it was moving. When I went inside it had a mouth.

Cameron Royston (6) Marayong South PS

I would be delighted if I had a MAGIC!! house and it had a water slide to get me down and an escalator to get me up. It would be exciting.

Sam James (6) Lismore PS

❧ THE MORNING GLORY ❧

We have morning glory growing all over the house. At the top of the house there is always a beautiful purple flower. I have got morning glory all around my window and all up the side of my bedroom.

Rigel hasn't got morning glory growing around his window. He has wild passionfruit growing up his side, and so has Leo.

We also have an old apple tree and it has morning glory growing all over it. I *LIKE* my house.

Lyra Butler (7) Coonabarabran PS

❧ MY FIVE RULES AT HOME ❧

1. You are allowed to leave the room a mess.
2. You are allowed to play SO much.
3. You and your friends can play noisily.
4. You are allowed to jump in the pool.
5. You can go down the back.

Sarah Andrews (7) Seven Hills West PS

THE DAY MY ROOM GOT PAINTED

After school I hopped off the bus, said Bye to Ennis, got an iceblock, went down the house and saw all my stuff in the hallway. I thought what are they doing to my room? I walked into my room and it was blue, it looked like the whole sky was trapped inside my room. Dad must've seen me walk into my room. He said, "Do you like it?" I didn't know what to say, I was completely speechless. I just didn't know what to say.

Bradley Wall (8) Jindabyne PS

MOVING TO MY NEW BEDROOM

Today Mum and I moved my bedroom and there was stuff everywhere. My bedroom floor was covered.

Mum started to move my little cupboard. She finally got it into my new bedroom. Then she pulled the big wardrobe to the step in my old bedroom. She tried to pull the wardrobe up the step. I was on the floor sweeping up the dust. Suddenly the wardrobe came flying down at me. I looked up and saw it. I tried to get out of the way but it was too late. The wardrobe hit my shoulder, Bang, but it did not hurt very much.

The wardrobe hit the floor with a crash but it was not broken.

Eventually Mum got the wardrobe up the step and into my new bedroom. Now I am sitting in my bedroom and when I go to bed I will be able to see the big moon shining through the window.

David White (8) Concord West PS

FAMILIES

My mum is pretty in her star dress. I help my mum with the washing up in the morning.

Thao Tran (6) Merrylands PS

It is my dad's birthday. He got a bottle of scotch. I gave him chocolate with peanuts. My sister gave him socks. I didn't give him peace and quiet to watch the news.

Darren Makin (6) Coonabarabran PS

THE EASTER HOLIDAY SHOW

I went to the Easter Holiday Show on 20th April, 1987. I sat in the cable car twice and it cost my Daddy to pay $4.00 for my trips. Daddy bought me a Barbie Show Bag, and my brother, Danny, had a Karate Kid Show Bag. Daddy and Danny went to sit on a gunny-sack to slide down on a big and colourful slide. On another ride, they sat in a little car which looked very dangerous. Mummy visited the farm sheds and said the cows were very smelly. Daddy disturbed a cock and a turkey, they got angry and wanted to bite my Daddy. Mummy said the chicken and duck were smelly too. We left the Show Ground at about 2.30 p.m.

Julie Choo (8) Arncliffe PS

🍃 ABOUT MY NAN'S LIFE 🍃

My nanna's name is Mrs Ross and she lives by herself in Camden and sometimes we go and visit her and sometimes she comes to our house. She loves to have naps in the daytime and she used to have a dog called Sandy but she died.

Sometimes Melissa or Susan sleep there and if I do I do the dishes for her and the housework. She is old and I feel sorry for her living alone, she has a beautiful garden in the front and back with vegetables growing, and she has a pet blue tongued lizard in the back garden.

She lives in a townhouse and the number is 12, she has a car and a roll up door and she has someone to come and clean the house.

She has a canary. She loves sewing and she has beautiful clothes and a collection of spoons and dolls. She also has heaps of albums and books.

That's all about my Nan. She's sweet.

Kim Paul (9) Claymore PS

🍃 AUTUMN LEAVES 🍃

Katrina looked up at her grandfather. He was reciting a poem and was getting really flared up. Katrina giggled — his teeth were nearly falling out.

Katrina's mother called her over. "You shouldn't laugh when Pop is reciting his poems. He takes them very seriously," she advised.

"I try not to but Pop looks so funny with his teeth falling out," Katrina told her.

"Well, try not to laugh — PLEASE!" her mother appealed.

"I'll try," Katrina said.

Later on as Katrina sat reading "Dolly", she thought back on what Mum had said and felt slightly guilty, but then she brushed her guilt aside. Pop criticised everything she did — the books that she read, her clothes, her music, her posters and her ideas. Why should SHE feel guilty?

Later on that night, Pop asked Katrina to go and sit in the loungeroom with him. When they were in the loungeroom, Pop looked at Katrina and began.

"Katrina, I know that I've been criticising you a lot lately but it's just that when I was your age, girls wore long dresses and were very properly taught at school."

Katrina looked down at her purple tank top and white mini-skirt and realised what Pop was trying to say.

"What I guess I'm trying to say, Katrina, is . . . I'm sorry!"

Katrina gave her grandfather a kiss on the cheek and went to bed.

Early next morning Katrina woke and went out of her room to find her mum and dad sitting in the kitchen. "Katrina — Pop's dead," her mother told her.

Katrina went back to her room and wouldn't let anyone in until her mother told her to get ready for the funeral. At the

"Abstracted Action"   *Greg Franklin (11) Normanhurst West PS*

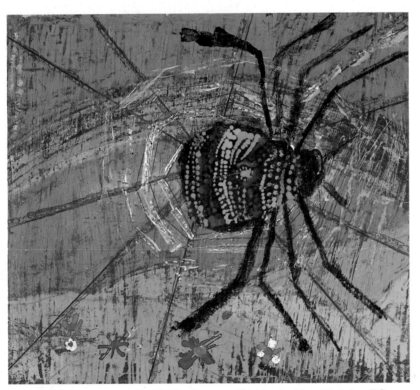

"Spider on a Web" *Kellie Burton (9) Newbridge Heights PS*

George Salagianis (9) Earlwood PS

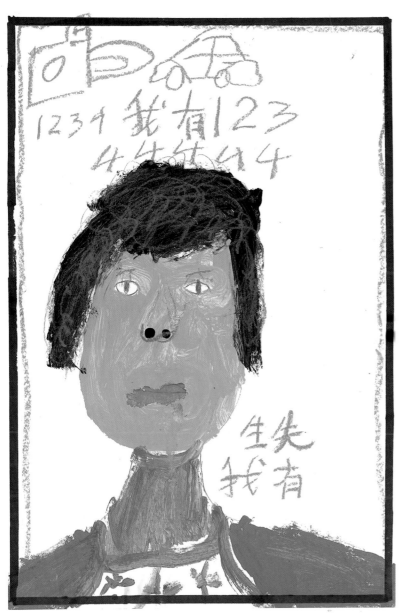

Year 6 (11) Balgowlah Heights PS

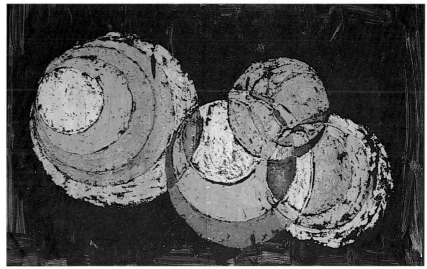

"Mrs Cohen"   *Cedric Cheuk (5) Artarmon PS*

Verity Coleman (11) Ulladulla PS

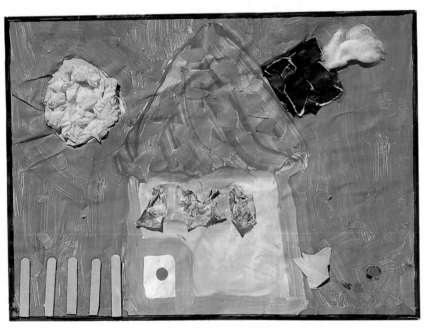

Millie Hofmann (6) Blackfriars Infants, Chippendale

Andrew Hobson (11) Dunedoo Central

funeral, as the minister was giving his sermon, Katrina could be heard whispering, "I'm sorry too, Pop."

Sarah Proudfoot (12) Deniliquin South PS

❧ I'M NOT ALLOWED TO ❧

I'm not allowed to sing loudly in the house but sometimes I have to practice. I'm not allowed to stay up late, but when my dad isn't there, my mum lets me. She is kind, isn't she? I'm not allowed to throw things around the room but sometimes when I am angry I cannot help it.

Kate Fennell (7) Ourimbah PS

❧ THE FEELING I GET WHEN I'M ANGRY! ❧

When I am angry I feel myself blasting out like a bomb, attacking streets, suburbs, towns, cities, states, countries, the world, planets and the whole universe. That's when my parents are shouting at me. BUT, my brother and my cousin David are even worse. I just feel like murdering them but I don't. I'll scream with rage if they annoy me and I really mean it. I hate, I just hate it when I get into trouble for screaming that loud, from my mum. She said that I was like a bomb but even louder. Didn't I get the big, big belt for doing that! I felt angry about that and I wanted to hit my mum back. I just didn't care about anything. I wouldn't dare do it or she'd do something nice that I wouldn't like. If anyone dared to say anything horrible about my mum I'd bash their face in. Only I can say that mum is not fair and is cruel. In the time when I am really angry I will swear words at anyone. I just don't care. I swear behind my mum's back and swear in front of my brother. I hold a knife and chase my brother around the house to scare him off but I don't throw it at him. If my brother was bashed up by a guy or two, I would feel sorry for my brother even if he had made me angry. I would always get the guy back for what he'd done to my brother if I could. That's all the feelings I get when I am angry. I cannot think of any other things that I would do to people when I am angry. I think that's enough!

Caroline Chieu (10) Auburn PS

❧ WHY ME? ❧

"Mum, Mum, where are you Mum?" screamed Vanessa.
"I'm in my bedroom," came the reply.
"Where are you going?" shrieked Vanessa.
"I'm going to the doctor's, I won't be long honey."
"But why, I can't see anything wrong with you," Vanessa screamed.
Her mother said, "Will you just be quiet for a minute. I'm already late, we'll talk later." The door slammed behind her.
"Oh no," huffed Vanessa, "I can't find my stupid book. Kylie!!! Have you seen my book?"
"Why don't you come up here and ask me?" Kylie screamed back. Vanessa ran up the twenty stairs to her sister's bedroom. When she finally reached it she found her sister in the closet talking to her boyfriend on the phone.
"Well, what do you want?" screeched Kylie. "You know that you have to knock before you barge in, anyway what do you want?"
"You told me to come up here to ask you something," replied Vanessa.
"Well can't you see I'm talking to someone very important. Now GET OUT!!!"

Vanessa's mum came home late when Vanessa was in bed. Her mum crept past her door quietly.

"Mum," whispered Vanessa.

"Yes honey," said her mother.

"Why did you have to go to the doctor's?"

"We'll talk about it in the morning, OK?"

Vanessa woke up worrying about what her mother had been doing behind her back. She walked into the kitchen. Kylie and her mum were already up.

"Mum," said Vanessa tiredly, "why did you have to go to the doctor's?"

"Come into the loungeroom and we'll talk about it."

"Well, Vanessa," said her mother, "I have some very good news for you."

"Well what is it?" Vanessa said sharply.

"You're going to have a little baby sister, isn't that just great news?" her mother said happily.

"No!" screamed Vanessa. "How could you Mum!"

"How could I what?" said her mother.

"You know."

"No. I don't know." Her mother's voice sounded angry.

"How could you and Dad carry on like that behind my back?" Vanessa ran to her room and slammed the door after her.

Vanessa's mum had her baby on the 21st February, while Vanessa was having French lessons. While Vanessa was walking home she thought about a little baby sister. She loved little kids but she knew she would be completely out of the family.

When she got to the front door she found her sister sitting on the couch with a book of baby's names. Her father was arguing with her. He was saying, "Kylie, we have already decided on the baby's name, end of argument."

"But Dad," whined Kylie, "don't you think Gabriel is sort of . . ." Kylie paused.

"Sort of what?" asked her father.

"Dumb," replied Kylie. "If somebody came up and said what is the little dear's name I'd be very embarrassed . . . Oh well, it looks like Vanessa and I will be stuck with saying that name for the rest of our lives."

Nerida Fagan (10) Engadine PS

❧ WHERE'S CARLIE? ❧

"Mum," I yelled. "Where's Carlie?"

"In her bedroom," she yelled back.

I went into Carlie's room but she wasn't there. I checked under the bed, behind the door and everywhere, so I went and told Mum.

"I had to ground her," she said. "I caught her out the back trying to break her new shoes, and she told me she hated everything in this world and she ran into her bedroom."

It was 7.00 p.m. and there was still no sign of her, so Mum rang the police. She had already checked with our relatives. All of a sudden, I remembered that I hadn't heard the dog barking since Carlie disappeared. I ran out the back but the dog had gone too.

"Here come the police," called Mum. We both ran out to meet them. Mum was talking ten to the dozen. We were just about ready to call a search party when along came Carlie and our dog. Mum ran to her not knowing whether to spank her or hug her. She ended up doing both!

Carlie had taken the dog for a walk without telling anyone, as if to pay Mum back for grounding her. We became really worried. Mum said that she wasn't allowed to go anywhere for two weeks so it didn't really work anyway.

Lisa Quast (11) North Albury PS

14

Kathleen Krnel (11) Concord PS

❧ A NEW ROOM ❧

Hi, my name is Chris. I live at 9, Talbot St, Riverwood and have to share a room with my 13 year old brother. I hate him. I wish I had a room of my own. Five reasons why I should have a new room.

1) My brother keeps smashing my old aeroplanes.
2) He won't turn on the TV of a morning.
3) He keeps taking my sheets of a night.
4) He won't stop talking about his dream girl.
5) I WANT A ROOM OF MY OWN.

Mum said, "Ask your father." So I asked Dad. He said, "Where do you think you're going to go?" I said, "The old study would be good." So that day I moved in. My brother helped by throwing my Jet Hopper. I stayed in that room for two boring weeks. It was so boring, nothing to do but sit around doing nothing. So I wrote a list. Five reasons why I should move back with Steven.

1) All of my messy models don't get smashed.
2) I don't mind turning on the TV of a morning.
3) I get boiling hot of a night.
4) I didn't get to hear the good bits about his dream girl.
5) I WANT TO MOVE BACK WITH STEVEN.

So I asked my Mum and Dad. They both said "Yes!" and Steven said "Yes." So that day I moved back into my old room.

Christopher Suttor (10) Peakhurst PS

❧ MOTHERS ARE ALWAYS RIGHT ❧

Here I am, 13 years old and NO mirror. A girl about my age NEEDS a mirror. Everyone in the house HAS a mirror — except me! When I want something, Mum says I am a nag; and the more I nag the less I get, and the less I nag the more I get. (If you know what I mean!) Anyway back to the mirror business. What does my brother do with his mirror? He never brushes his hair. All he ever does is stare at himself! What does my baby sister do with her mirror? NOTHING! Absolutely NOTHING! I need one. Example: to brush my hair, to see how many freckles are still there, so I know if I look colour-coordinated, and all that junk.

I came home from school the next day and the first thing I asked Mum was: "Have you got my mirror yet?" Then she went off into a screaming session about how I nag. She reckoned I wanted all these things:

hi-fi system
watch
Bangles album
book on how to draw
new carpet
poster of M.J. Fox
footy jumper
shoes
new quilt cover
and last but not least a
MIRROR.

Mum's right, I *am* a nag.

Jodi Waller (11) Mt Brown PS

SCHOOLS

❧ SPEECH FOR SCHOOL CAPTAIN ❧

Ding Dong Ding Dong Big Ben calling!
I will keep the school from falling.
In my speech I said I'd do
Everything I can for you,
To keep St Jo's respected name
And bring it academic fame.

I'll play with you, I'll pray for you
And try to show the way for you.
I'll be your brother and your friend
Until my sixth-grade days shall end.
Now, VOTE FOR ME! and you will see
How really great the school can be!

Ben Ellis (11) St Joseph's, Coraki

I wish I was a tiger. I would not have to do school work. I could growl at people and if I went in to the school the children would run away.

Luke Gollan (6) Coonabarabran PS

❧ THE FIRST DAY OF FIFTH GRADE 1987 ❧

. . . I was walking down Aubrey Street and thinking what teacher I could get this year. I was in Cumberland Road, now I crossed the road, strolled up a long path, crossed at the lights, sprinted down another path and skidded in the gate of the school. Aaaahhh. I had arrived at school. I looked at my watch, it was 8.10 a.m. and I had woken up at 8 a.m. I couldn't believe it. It was the earliest I had ever been. Everyone at school was nervous. I could tell my friend Amy was nervous because when I let her have a look at my Pound Puppy Newborn, she kept twiddling his ears. She was also saying that she was nervous. We were all shaky because we desperately wanted to know what teacher we were getting.

My friends and I had absolutely nothing to do so we sat down and talked about our holidays. It sounded like everybody had had a good holiday. We had finished talking when the bell rang. We lined up in our old classes excitedly, and then the teacher said "Forward over to the assembly area." In our old classes we sat down on the silver seats. The first teacher to call out her class was Mrs Bopping. She is a funny teacher, but I really wanted to be in Mrs McClure's class. Mrs Bopping was calling out the boys in her class and the only boys I knew in her class are Shane Bugg and Samuel Bruin. Now she was calling the girls in her class. First she said Ann Maree Beeton and then she said Nicole Broughton. She was nearly to the end of the list when she said Danielle Wiggins. I was so happy that my best, best friend was in my class again, but all of a sudden Mrs McClure came over and told Danielle that she is in her class now and she will swap her with Natalie Hopper. Now I was sad, I was so sad that I nearly cried. I thought that I had no friends in 5B but I found that I had Rebecca Roberts, Wendy Lukzti and Rhiannon Sewell and I soon made part-time friends with Angela Johnson.

We rushed into our new classroom and sat on the carpet and just talked about the people in our class. Soon it was little lunch and I rushed up to Amy and said "How do you like your new teacher Amy?" She said "Oh, I like him a lot now, I think he's cool." At little lunch all Danielle and I did was talk to people about their class. The bell rang and we lined up in our new class. At first I was a bit puzzled as to where I had to line up, but I just had to look for the people in my class. After we stood outside for at least five minutes we dawdled into our classroom. We spent an hour and a half working and then the bell rang again to pack up. When it was 3 p.m. we all rushed out of the classroom, grabbed our bag and ran down the stairs and walked home. When I got home I told my mum all about my first day of 5th grade, and I said I had a really good day.

Nicole Broughton (11) Ingleburn PS

❧ THE USUAL BORING SPELLING LESSON ❧

"Bicycle . . . b-i-c-y-c-l-e. Successful . . . s-u-c-c-e-s-ZZzzzzzz."

Our new carpet is nice, but I'd like it better when it hasn't got all the fluff balls on it.

"Sorry, Mr Butler. Yes, I'll pay attention in future."

Mr Butler has gone to the store-room but he's come out as soon as he went in.

My cousin Ben moved to Grafton last month. I wish he could stay.

"Great . . . g-r-e-a-t."

Ben's dad works with the DMR. Dad works with computers. He's a programmer. There's a computer in the classroom now.

I can't wait until we go to Sydney for the day.

"Accommodation . . . a-c-c- " Oh! who cares how you spell it! We might go to Sydney Tower for the second time. It's so high that Mum doesn't dare go and look out the windows. We went for a joy flight in a light aircraft for an hour. It was great.

It'll be great when I get home because my favourite show, Wheel of Fortune, will be on. I like watching TV, it's fun because some of the shows are really exciting.

"Happy . . . h-a-p-p-y."

A man with a trolley has just come into our room with one of our heaters on it. It looks really funny. We might get a new heater for home this winter. Another heater has just come into the room on the trolley. It looks just as funny as the one before.

"Yes, Mr Butler. I do deserve detention because I'm day-dreaming."

I think I'll buy the Garfield book from book club. Tim has a few Garfield books at home. That's why I'll buy it.

"Pursue . . . p-u-r-s-u-e."

I also want the Eyespy Magazine. It sounds interesting and I always enjoy them. The two books are both from Star on the orange paper. I also like ice-cream, mmmmm.

"ANDREW FRASER. PAY ATTENTION! YOU'RE ON DETENTION TWICE NOW! I shouldn't have to talk to you again today!"

"Thorough . . . t-h-o-r-o-u-g-h . . . jewel . . . j-e-w-e-l . . . occasion . . . o-c-c-a-s- . . . ZZZZZzzzzzzz . . . ZZZZZZZZZZzzzzzzzzzz."

Andrew Fraser (9) Glenbrook PS

The class lined up in two straight lines
And we walked to Rickaby's Creek
We carried our pencils in our hand
And we wore shoes upon our feet.

We stood beside the murky brown pond
Mrs Coulter and the class
There were lily pads and the sun shone
We could hear rustling grass.

We saw back swimmers, ducks and pelicans too
Guppies and moss and reeds
And a boy from Mr Cooper's class
Found an awful looking leech.

We wandered around the edge of the pond
To find a spot to draw
Then in the grass we sat and drew
Pictures of wonderful things we saw.

Then once again in two straight lines
We walked back to the school
To Mr Cooper's room we went
And we talked of our afternoon.

It was a lovely thing to do
On a sunny day in May
To wander beside the pond
Then walk back to school again.

Tareese Evans (8) South Windsor PS

THE ARMY FUNERAL

The army funeral was very sad. I nearly burst into tears and
Monsignor Harley said the Mass. We saw all the soldiers
marching by our school. The Band played slow, sad music and
we saw hundreds of beautiful coloured flowers and Monsignor
was in the Army and he was marching with another man, and
then the music started again and the school children were all
watching all of the soldiers marching down Cardinal Street, and
police were stopping the traffic coming near Cardinal Street
and hundreds and thousands of school children saw the funeral.
The cars were black and there were nine cars, and some white
cars were coming behind the soldiers, and they were going
slowly. The soldiers had guns in their hands, and they didn't
blink at all. Also we saw the person dying in the coffin; there
were beautiful flowers around the coffin. I hope that their soul
goes to heaven tonight. Cardinal Street was blocked off. No
cars were allowed to go through it. We watched the soldiers
marching past. Then we went back to class. The big band was
playing and singing when we went back to class they were
singing sad songs.

Daniel Street (6) Sacred Heart, Mosman

SOUNDS IN THE CLASSROOM

Still.
Stillness.
Nothingness in the air.
Air wisping through the windows.
The teacher's pen writing homework sheets.
Children's soft voices creeping through the whole school.
Chalk dropping and sliding across the floor,
While footsteps clump up and down to sharpen their pencils.
A bag falls off the rack and makes the stillness louder.
The bell rings and everything is stillness and nothingness again,
While children's shadows
Glide across the school yard.

Fiona Jensen (8) New Lambton PS

HAPPENINGS

🐦 MRS BORING 🐦

I have got a next door neighbour and she is boring. Her name is Mrs Baker. She sits around all day and does nothing. One day Jessica and I went knick knocking on her door. Then we hid behind a bush. We kept knocking on her door until she gave up sitting around all day.

Fiona Davey (8) Mulwala PS

🐦 A COUNTRY FAIR 🐦

I had just arrived at the show. I could see people sweating and children eating icecreams. I heard screams and the champion ram bleating. I smelt foul rubbish and food. Then I went on the roller coaster. I felt nervous and scared. It was the best day of my life. I asked if we could come next year!

Tony Scott (8) Sandy Beach PS, Woolgoolga

Yesterday mum said to go to the kitchen, but when I got there I saw a little grey mouse. Our cat was chasing it. I called mum. She came quickly and she got that mouse out. But that night it came back and mum didn't know. So the mouse ate all our cheese. Mum was very mad. So I killed it. Mum bought some more cheese. No more mice bothered us. That was good.

Rebecca Hall (5) Cooma North PS

🐦 THE BIRD 🐦

A bird swooped down on me. He missed me by about this much.

Brett Lackey (6) Coonabarabran PS

I went to Denims Beach and I went in the surf. I also visited the sawmill. After that we went to the place where cheese is made. We saw the machines stirring the milk to make the curds and whey. They drain the whey into containers to feed the pigs. The men press the curds into square tins. In four months this is cheese. We saw the big block of cheese sliced in a machine. Then a big machine wrapped the cheese in strong plastic for the supermarket.

Gwilym Griffiths (6) Turramurra North PS

One weekend I went to a barbeque. Guess how much I ate? I ate six sausages, ten drinks, one pork spare rib and two pieces of steak. Can you imagine, I didn't get fat!

Tara White (5) Cooma North PS

❧ MY TOOTH ❧

My tooth is wriggly. It is about to come out. In school it came out. That night the fairy came. I got a dollar. One day when one of my other teeth came out I had it on the table in a glass and mum was looking for dirty glasses and she picked up the glass with my tooth in it and washed it up and my tooth went down the sink and when the fairy came I got two dollars.

Belinda Morgan (7) Kurri Kurri PS

Once upon a time when I went to bed, I dreamed a scary dream and there were dinosaurs and I dreamed that I was in it and I hid behind a tree so the dinosaurs would not get me. My mum and dad woke me up in the morning and I told them all about my dream.

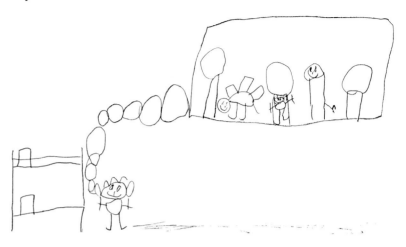

Ezra Murray (5) Covenant Christian School, Belrose

I am frightened of the dark and I get my dolls and put them under my covers and have a meeting.

Jocelyn Cole (6) Seven Hills West PS

❧ MY TREASURE ❧

My treasure is Pinky. Pinky is my security blanket. He used to be pink and fluffy. He is grey and holey but I don't care, because I've had him since I was 3 months old. My Godmother gave him to me. In 1985 she bought me a new one. I called it Emergency Blanket, but I've only used it once. I suck my

One night when I was
so little I heard a noise
as something was creeping
on my roof. I was
wondering what it was
and I was not frightened
of it but it <u>was</u> <u>loud.</u>
My mum and dad woke
up with a terrible fright
because they did not
know what it was.
They put on the light.
What is that loud noise.
They jumped up on the bed.
"Oh dear" mum and dad said.
That thing said "Oh dear I am
sick today."

Lynda Duncan (6) Abbotsford PS

finger and fluff it even though people say that there's nothing on it but they must be blind. I get heaps of fluff (even enough to fill a room, well, not as much). I take it to bed with me to help me sleep and in the morning I wake up with it in my hands. I gave Emergency Blanket to Tootsie my dog. She loves it!!

Anne Eburn (10) Leura PS

❧ ABOVE THE SKY ❧

One night as I was sleeping I had a dream that I was above the sky surrounded by creatures. I had drawn these at school, I can tell you they were ugly, an uncountable number of eyes looking upon me. The creatures had slimy skin, horns and four legs each. I was held captive with other human beings. I remembered I had lots of gold in my pockets so I decided I would try to pay my way out. Courageously I offered it but they refused to take it. I tried everything I could think of. Then I remembered that if I could dream I was at school I could erase them. I tried to sleep, without success. All of a sudden I had an idea maybe I could dance my way out! I persuaded the creatures to let me dance. In my costume I started dancing to the music. As I was dancing they let everybody go except me. I began screaming. I turned around and I realised I was back home, with my friends staring at me.

Tracie Seipel (9) St Joseph the Worker, Auburn South

22

OUTDOORS

At the weekend I learned how to ride a bike. I could hold on well and could do anything. I could go fast.

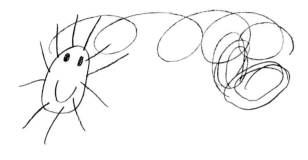

Guy Lawrence (7) Maroubra Junction PS

Snow is glittering and when you ski down the slopes it makes a chooming noise and I like it. There is ice on the snow too. But, you wouldn't ski if you didn't know how. Snow is just too beautiful. It doesn't matter just wherever you ski, whether you ski in Perisher, Thredbo or any other resort.

When I was skiing with my ski teacher I skied over a great big ski jump. It was fun and it was sunny. And I really, really loved it a lot and it was so fun that I did it over and over again, and, the next day I did it much more.

Hamish MacDonald (6) Jindabyne PS

❧ THE EXCITEMENT OF CATCHING A WAVE ❧

I was out the back
past the rest
you could clearly see
that I was the best
　　Upon that wave
I would ride
with nobody else
by my side.

　　King of the surf
that was me
oh what fun
oh what glee
　　Then suddenly
before I knew
I saw a wave
start to brew.

　　It was the biggest wave
I ever saw
no wonder people
dropped their jaw

They said "Oh My!
Oh deary me!
Will she ride
that mighty sea?"

Of course I did
with spray in my face
but I didn't care
I was with the pace
    Through that tube
I shot like a rocket
I didn't miss even
one small pocket.

    I slid out the end
with lots of ease
I caught that wave
like a breeze
    Then on that wave
I did a 360
you could see I
was very nifty.

    I rode that wave
right into shore
I didn't think
it was a bore
    It's something now
that I crave
the exhilaration
of catching a wave.

Kate Cooper (11) Bilgola Plateau PS

❧ FISHING ❧

I've fished in the river,
I've fished in the sea.
I've fished before breakfast,
And long after tea.

I can honestly say
That of fishing I'm fond,
But I caught my best fish
In the old village pond.

Its scales were pure silver,
Its fins were bright gold.
Its tail rainbow coloured
A joy to behold.

It gazed at me sadly,
With its eyes jet black.
It looked so unhappy,
I threw it straight back.

Natalie Hicks (11) Macksville PS

❧ NETBALL ❧

We watch the captains go out for the call
It looks like our centre has won the ball!
We maintain our position till the hooter sounds
The centre passes, it rolls out of bounds
The game is close and the tension high

My skinned leg hurts so much I feel I could cry
With seconds to go the scores all tied up
The ball must go in to win us the cup
The ball's in the air, it circles the ring,
At last it comes down, Hey! bingo it's in!

Stephanie Potts (12) Dubbo South PS

❧ From THE FOOTY MATCH ❧

It is Sunday afternoon — 3.00 p.m. The crowd is cheering and booing the two teams that are going to play the next game at Leichhardt Oval. The players run on to the field — first Parramatta, then Balmain . . .

"Who are you betting on today?" I ask my friend Rob who is helping me in the commentator's box.

"Ah! I don't know really," he answers.

This year Parramatta has won ten games and so have the Tigers.

"I'm betting on the Tigers. Who are you betting on, Jim?" I ask another commentator.

"I'm betting on Parramatta," he says and the referee's whistle goes to start the game.

Mick Cronin takes the kick-off. Garry Jack takes the catch, run the ball up ten metres until he's tackled. He gets it out to Hemsley, on to Conlon, out to Bridge but it is intercepted by Peter Sterling.

Sterling is tackled on the Balmain quarter line. Sterling gets it out to Wynn, out to Ella. Ella is out of one tackle, out of two, he is going to score in front of the posts but Garry Schofield shows a magnificent performance and tackles Steve Ella one metre out from the posts. "That was beautiful playing," I

shouted into the microphone. "Garry Schofield has been one of the stars this year for Balmain."

Ella plays the ball to Jurd. Jurd passes it out to Sharp and he is tackled but gets the ball out to Liddiard. He is tackled three metres out from Balmain's line.

Jurd passes to Cronin. Cronin puts the bomb up. "Ella is going for it." Rob's voice is getting excited. "He catches it beautifully and dives across the line. Ella scores. Beautiful playing there by Ella. Four-nil Parramatta's way." Rob is so excited that he jumps out of his chair.

"Cronin will take the conversion," Rob says calmly. "He lines it up, walks back, runs, the kick looks good but it just misses. There goes the half-time siren. Gee that was quick," says Rob . . .

I take up the commentary as the end of the game approaches. "Roach passes to Gale. Gale puts in a chip. Jack looks like he might score. He's running. He is leaving the Balmain team behind and the Parramatta backs are nowhere near him. He's getting close to the line. He's crossed the line between the posts. Yes, Jack makes the score Parramatta – 4, Balmain – 4.

"While we wait for Conlon to take the conversion we will go across to the S.C.G. to see how Canberra and St George are going." The score at the Sydney Cricket Ground is, St George – 20, Canberra – 1.

When the broadcast comes back to Leichhardt Oval Balmain is 6, Parramatta is 4. I start the commentary, "During the break Ross Conlon kicked the conversion and there goes the full time siren. Balmain has beaten Parramatta by two points. Ladies and Gentlemen it has been an exciting match between Balmain and Parramatta. We all agree that Conlon is Man of the Match."

Nicholas Hayes (8) Concord West PS

FRIENDS

❧ WHAT'S A FRIEND? ❧

What's a friend? A friend is someone you play with. A friend is someone who never fights with you. A friend always helps you. I have a friend! Her name is Nicole! She has red hair and green eyes. She has freckles and is very pretty. I have lots of other friends. I'll tell you their names. They are Rachel and Jasmine. Rachel has dark hair and brown eyes. Jasmine has light brown hair and it is very long too. She has green eyes. They sparkle.

Michelle Rogers (7) Maroubra Junction PS

❧ WINTER GAMES ❧

I like playing with my friends.
We like playing in the snow.
My friends like making snowmen.
I just like playing.

Mathew Quirk (6) Narrabri PS

❧ CHASING SPACE MONSTERS ❧

"You can be a space policeman trying to catch a ferocious Martian. I'll be the Martian and I'll put on Uncle Bernie's space helmet. I'm ugly and slimy and very dangerous," explained Johnny to Rory. Rory was an imaginary friend which Johnny and his great imagination had created. "Count to one million and five while I run and hide. And Rory, keep practising your talking. It's terribly difficult to know whether you understand anything if you don't say so." And with that, Johnny went and hid.

Johnny was four years old. People often said that he used too many big words and let his imagination run wild, so Johnny had made friends with Rory as Rory didn't say anything. The broom cupboard was Johnny's favourite place to hide as Rory never thought of looking there, but today he decided not to hide there as the mothballs in the cupboard were beginning to smell. Instead he hid behind an enormous vase that was sitting next to his toy chest.

"There he is," said Johnny quietly to himself while peering round the edge of the vase. "Oh, no, he's coming this way." Quickly Johnny rushed out from behind the vase and on his way knocked the vase over and smashed it to smithereens. Johnny didn't worry about that. He climbed into the toy chest and crouched there as still as a mouse. He heard a door close and his mother's voice.

"Oh, no, what has happened to this vase? Jonathon Bignell, do you know what happened to it? Come on out. I know you are hiding somewhere."

"Boy," Johnny whispered, "Mum must be really mad. She never calls me Jonathon unless she's mad." He quietly crept out of the basket that his toys were in and walked over to his mother.

"Rory made me knock it over 'cause he was chasing me and I had to get away before he caught me, otherwise I would have had to go to gaol."

"Who on earth is Rory?" Mrs Bignell asked.

"Rory is my best friend and we were playing chase the space monster."

"Well, you can stop playing chase the monster and help me tidy up this mess."

"Oh, Mum, do I have to?" sulked Johnny.

"Either that or you can go and play hide-and-seek with the nice little girl next door."

"I'll help tidy up this mess." Johnny hated the girl next door.

After Johnny had tidied up the shattered vase he decided that he wouldn't have Rory as a best friend any more. Clearing up vases was tiring work. He'd create a nice quiet friend who enjoyed playing cowboys and Indians.

What could get broken playing cowboys and Indians?

Melissa Bell (10) Scone PS

❧ THE NEW BOY IN OUR STREET ❧

He was small, tiny, a midget.
His hair was blonde or white
He was shy or scared.
I like him, I think.
His mum is fat and ugly.
My mum is thin and beautiful.
His dad is thin and bony.
My dad is thin but not bony.
He goes to my school.
He's in my class.
I like him.
I went to his house.
He likes me!

Robert Sawyer (11) Our Lady of the Rosary, Shelly Beach

❧ TU ❧

Tu was a special friend of mine when I went to Unanderra Public School. She was Chinese, her mother was Chinese as well and her father was Japanese.

When I first started at that school Tu had no friends at all. She sat alone in class, but then I had to sit next to her. I found out that she was a very friendly girl.

When I was stuck with my work she always offered to help.

Soon it was Tu's birthday and I was invited to her party. I had longer hair then. For the party my hair was in ringlets. I gave Tu two cane dolls to sit on her dressing table.

Tu received many other lovely presents as well.

Third class passed quickly and soon I left Unanderra School and came to Cootamundra.

I had no Tu to talk to when I needed her. I always wonder if she has any friends at school any more.

I have Shandell now. She helps too. I like Shandell a lot. It's great having friends. It was lovely having a friend like Tu.

Skye Sargent (10) E.A. Southee PS, Cootamundra

❧ WHEN I WAS A BOY IN LAOS ❧

When I was a little boy in Laos I don't really remember much, but I do remember when my friend cut my hand with a shaving knife.

I was crying. When my Mum came home from work she asked, "What is that bandage around your arm?"

I didn't answer my Mum.

She came up close to me and asked again, looking at my arm, "Who did this? Was it that boy you're always playing with?"

"Y-y-y-y-yes, Mum."

So my Mum went to my friend's house and spoke to his Mother.

"Is your son home?"

"Yes. What do you want with him?"

"Look at what he's done to my son."

My friend's Mother looked at my arm.

"Poor boy . . . I'll get my son for you."

She went in to my friend's room. He came and talked to my Mum. She sounded angry. (I could hear her while I was watching television.)

After that my friend started hating me.

But I found a new friend. I made a tree house with him.

ຫລັງຈາກນັ້ນ ໝູ່ຂອງຂ້ອຍ ເກີດ ຄຽດແຄ້ນ ຂ້ອຍ .

ແຕ່ວ່າ ຂ້ອຍໄດ້ ໝູ່ ໃໝ່ດີໃໝ່ . ຂ້ອຍໄດ້ ຫຸ້ນ ເຮືອນ
ນ້ອຍ ຕົວນັ້ນ .

Neramith Insixiengmay (11) St Anthony's, Wanniassa

ຕາມ ຄວາມຈຳແລ້ວ ຂ້ອຍ ຢູ່ຄ່ອຍ ຄ: ຈ້ ອ້ຳໄດ້ ຫລາຍ ຢ່າງໃດ ໃນເວລາ
ຂ້ອຍ ຢູ່ ເປັນ ເດັກ ນ້ອຍ ຢູ່ ເຫັວລາວ , ຂ້ອຍ ຄ້ຳໄດ້ ປ່າ ນມາ ເວລາ
ໝູ່ ຂ້ອຍ ເຮົາ ມັກ ແກ ກ້າ ຢ່າ ໄຊ ຂ້ອຍ .

ຂ້ອຍໄດ້ ຮ້ອງໃຫ້ ເປັນ ຫມາໃນຍ . ເວລາ ແມ່ ຂ້ອຍ ຄັບ ມາ
ຈາກ ເຮັດ ອອກ ແມ່ ຖາມ ຂ້ອຍ ວ່າ " ເປັນ ຫຍັງ ເຈົ້າຈ່ ້ ຢ້າ ພັນ
ແຂນ ຢູ່ ແຂນເຈົ້າ ? " ຂ້ອຍ ຈຶງ ໄດ້ ຕອບ ແມ່ ແຕ່ ປັງ ໃດ . ແມ່ ຂ້ອຍ
ຈັບ ເຈົ້າ ພາໃຫ້ ແລະ: ເປີດ ເບິ່ງ ແຂນຂ້ອຍ ແລ; ຖາມ ຂ້ອຍ ອີກ ວ່າ:
" ຜ່ໃດ ເຮັດ ນີ ? ເດົາ ມ້ອງ ຄົມ ຫ້ ເຄີຍ ຫລັງ ໃຫ້ເຈົ້າ ບ່ ເຮົ້ອ ໆ ແນ່ ,
ອໍ່ ? " ບ . " ແມ່ ! ແມ່ ! ແມ່ ມາແລ້ວ ແມ່ !

ແມ່ ຂ້ອຍ ໂ ້ ໆ ໄປ ຫ້ ້ ເຮືອນ ໝູ່ ຂອງ ຂ້ອຍ ແລະ: ເຈົ້າ ກັບ ແມ່
ຂອງ ເຈົ້າ: " ລູກ ຊາຍ ເຈົ້າ ຢູ່ ເຮືອນ ບ່ ? " ບ່ຢູ່ ເຈົ້າ ຢາກ ເຮັດ ຫຍັງ ກັບ ນັ້ນ ? "
" ເບິ່ງ ນ່ ດູ , ລູກ ຊາຍ ເຈົ້າ ເຮັດ ຫຍັງ ກັບ ລູກຊາຍ ຂ້ອຍ ." ແມ່ ຂອງ ໝູ່ ຂ້ອຍ
ໄດ້ ເບຍ ບິ່ງ ແຂນ ຂ້ອຍ : " ໂອ ! ໝ່າ ລູກ ຊາຍ .... ຂ້ອຍ ຈະ ໄປ ເອົາ ເຈົ້າ
ຊາຍ ລູກ ຂ້ອຍ ມາ ." ແມ່ ລູກ ໝູ່ ຂ້ອຍ ໄດ້ ເຈົ້າ ໄປ ໃນ ນ່ຫ້ . ໝູ່ ຂ້ອຍ
ໄດ້ ອອກ ມາ ເຈົ້າ ກັບ ແມ່ ຂ້ອຍ . ແມ່ ຂ້ອຍ ໃຈ ໃຈ ຮ້າຍ . (ຂ້ອຍໄດ້ ບນ
ຮູ້ ເວລາ ຂ້ອຍ ກ່າ ລາ ບ້ຳ (ໂທລະ ທັດ) .

❧ YESTERDAY ❧

You and I were friends yesterday.
East and west we went together.
So now I'm alone.
The things we did together!
Exciting coming up the hill
Riding on our bikes.
Day after day going by.
Are we ever going to be friends again?
Yes, we are!

Alison Howard (6) Avondale SDA Primary, Cooranbong

❧ A DEAD FRIEND ❧

The thunder struck.
The lightning split the sky.
She's dead.
Call the ambulance 000.
Too late — she's dead.
Oh no — it can't be true.
Why?
Tell me why did she have to die?

Isaac Jahn (9) Newbridge Heights PS

Aaron Smith (11) Wamberal PS

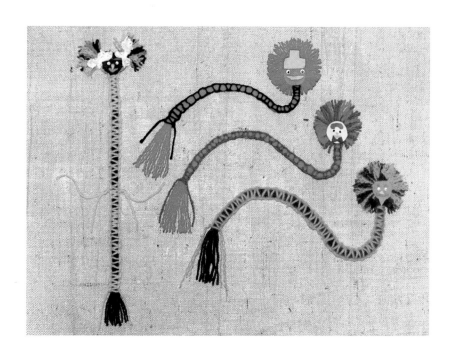

Linocuts   *Year 6 MLC, Burwood*

◄   Macrame   *Jemma Clark (10) Travers Wood (10)*
Diana Alley (10) Matthew Bramley (10) Dural PS

Kites   *Karen Jones (6) Nicole Podmore (6) Faulconbridge PS*   *Jude Fernandez (10) Earlwood PS*

It's just not fair.
Did you hear me? It's just not fair.

A week has passed.
Life is miserable without this special someone by your side.
I feel all jumpy and nervous.
I can't even go to her funeral.
I wouldn't like to die the way she died the way of darkness.
Even the sigh of the wind reminds me of her death.

Nicola Jockel (10) Kororo PS

❧ A LETTER TO HEAVEN ❧

Sunshine spilled into the half vacant room, waking its occupant and the small geranium. The small child stirred between the two pushed together chairs.

A table, two chairs, a sink, a cupboard and a gold locket were all she owned. She did not know how to spell but could read with difficulty.

One day, a while ago, she had asked a drunk what her name was. His words were slurred, but she worked out that her first name was Lacey.

When her Mama was dying, a relative had taken her away. She had been passed from aunts to uncles, from cousins to friends. The longest she had stayed anywhere was Rosie's house. Rosie pretended to be good but when her husband was gone, which was often, she would tie Lacey to a chair and throw food at her. Once a brick was thrown at her for bringing in a stray cat.

A man called Pete found her and took her home, but she trusted no one until Sam. Sam was an old man who was as lonely as she was ugly. The brick incident had left her half blind with a limp. Sam did not have much but he gave her what he had.

Two days? Had it been only two days ago that her only friend had fallen in the mall and died? She did not cry. She simply walked away. Sam . . . Time to go to the shops.

She straightened her dress and set out. In an empty aisle she took three cans of beans. The caretaker came around the corner, saw her and chased her out of the shop. He caught her, making her wince with pain.

"I's gotten you now, thiefy!"

Lacey's mouth tightened as he pushed her into the view of others.

"Who owns this scoundrel?" he asked.

After some hesitation a balding man came forward and claimed her as his. His warm fingers touched hers as she walked forward ready to be hurt again. He took her home, fed her soup and put her in a bed.

After five weeks of schooling she knew how to write the simplest things. Then she decided to let her past be past and she began to enjoy the love that was given to her. Then she thought of telling her old friend about her new life.

> Dear Sam,
> I am happy. You were good to me and now Mr Kase is good to me.
>> Love always,
>> Lacey.

It was a simple letter, yet it was honest. The most natural things in the world are honesty, truth and love.

Danielle Manning (12) Scone PS

PETS

My dog is 6 months old. She came from the R.S.P.C.A. Her name is Mitzi. Mum gets cross with her when she pulls the washing off the line.

Alison Hicks (5) Padstow North PS

When I bought my dog my mum said I may not keep it. She doesn't like dogs. He went back to the shop.

Iva Kvesic (6) Seven Hills West PS

My dog went to the firecrackers. He was scared. I wasn't. He went next to me. He was silly.

Luke Kendall (5) St Mary's, Wellington

At home I have two pet cats. Their names are Kitty and Pussy. I like to play with Kitty. I don't play with Pussy, because she does not like to be picked up by anybody. Pussy is grey and Kitty is all kinds of colours. I like my cats a lot. I used to have ten fish and I fed them fish-food every day after school. But we sold them to a man with two children.

Kathryn Hume (6) St Patrick's, Asquith

❧ ESHA ❧

She followed my footsteps
in the garden
where she laid her head,
fading away
in a pile of dirt.

We made a cross,
with her name engraved.
I remember the good times,
she would play with me
for hours.

She would lay on my bed,
and fall asleep.
I regret the times
I was bad to her.

I loved Esha – so very much.

Mima Dietrich (10) St Mary's, Liverpool

❧ WHITE RABBITS ❧

I like white Rabbits because they are soft cute and furry. They live in the bush in a burrow. I wish I had one for a pet.

I see them in pet shops but mum won't get me one because she thinks they are too expensive.

I like the way their ears stand up, the colour of their noses and how they twitch.

I never see them in the bush because they hide when they
see me, because they are terrified.

Peta Large (7) Wyoming PS

❧ DINOSAUR ❧

If you found a Dinosaur would you give him roses to eat?
Would you bath him every night? Would you take him for a
walk? If you found a Dinosaur would you show him to your
parents? If you found a Dinosaur would you hide him in a pot?
If I found a Dinosaur I would gather quite a few and start a pre-
historic zoo.

David Inglis (7) Murwillumbah East PS

❧ MY BIRD ❧

My bird is white with a yellow crest. Her name is Shelly.
Sometimes she's a pest and sometimes she's not. She eats
paddy and oranges and rice and potatoes. She pecks very hard
and you can get hurt. Sometimes when I feed her, she pecks me
and I scream. She loves my dad, and when she is allowed to
come out, she always goes onto my dad's shoulder and my dad
tries to get her off. Shelly flies when the fan is on and I scream
because I love her, and I don't want her to get hurt. When my
dad gives her a bath, I watch him, because when Shelly comes
out of the bath, she shivers like mad. I tell my dad to wrap her
up in a towel and my dad does. Occasionally she gets tangled
up and suddenly her head pops out and I get a fright, I then start
laughing. Most of the time, my dad likes to see her yellow crest
come up so he says "Perky up Shell". Sometimes she screeches
and my daddy gets mad. He locks her in a room and doesn't let
anyone go there. When she's quiet, he brings her out and
sometimes lets her come out of her cage. He usually tells me
not to go near her because she doesn't like kids. Sometimes
when Shelly flies, she settles down on my head. I get frightened
because I think she is going to peck me.

I love Shelly and I think she's the best bird ever.

Llana Menezes (9) Cronulla PS

❧ MY UNFORGETTABLE DOG ❧

My unforgettable dog had to be put down. Her name was
Deefer. Deefer had to be put down because she couldn't control
her bladder and had no feeling in her back legs. Deefer was
black and had brown eyes like me. Every time it rained we let
her come in on a towel. Every time I ran into my bedroom she
would come to the hallway door. I remember Deefer, because
she was a playful dog and a fast runner. The whole family cried
when the day came for Deefer to be put down.

Nathan Jamieson (9) Bexley North PS

❧ THAT DAY I CAME HOME ❧

That day I came home
I wish I wasn't there.
My puppy died.
The sight so gruesome
I couldn't help but stare.
It was lying down flat
Looking up at the wall.
Not a stir in its body
Just still and small.

I wish I could turn the day back.
As the tears began to flow
I asked myself
Why did it happen.
The answer
I don't know.

That day I wish I wasn't there
That day I came home.

Zoe Koulouris (9) New Lambton PS

❧ MICE ON HOLIDAY ❧

I'm going to write you a true story about two mice named Mickey and Squeek.

When I was 6 years old I was in first class and we had two pet mice in our class. All the students loved them and looked after them. So I decided that I would give them a good time and take them for a holiday.

I asked my mummy if I could bring them home and I was allowed to do so.

So I got up early in the morning and prepared the special cheese dish for them and went to school. I was very excited the whole day long. At 3 o'clock my mummy came to pick us up. Mickey and Squeek sat with me in the front seat very happy. My brother and sisters were waiting at the door for us and they all sang welcome, welcome, welcome.

The next day of our Easter holiday we took them to Hungerford Hill and they enjoyed the fresh air and a ride in the carriage.

Every day I cleaned their house and fed them lots and lots of cheese. At the end of our holiday all our neighbours and our family came to the car and said goodbye to them. They had a very thankful smile on their faces. Indeed they had a wonderful holiday.

I hope you like my story.

Asif Khan (7) Cessnock West PS

We caught a bird in our classroom and Shane was holding it.

The bird tried to fly away when we put it in the ice-cream container. It had a piece of glass in its foot. It looked as if it was bleeding. Mrs Velez pulled the glass out.

We took it outside to let it go. When we put it on the ground it flew away.

It was colourful too and I felt sad that we couldn't keep it.

Naomie O'Keeffe (6) Tregear PS

❧ HERMIT THE CRAB ❧

Last Sunday, our teacher, Miss King found a shell on her favourite beach. Inside the shell was a crab. Miss King brought him to school on Monday. Debby, one of the girls in our class, called him Hermit. We agreed upon the name.

We put him in a big see-through jar. He had lots of space to walk and scurry. Everyone in the class crowded around the jar to look at Hermit. He was very interesting. He hid himself under the shells and buried himself in the sand. He was very frightened, terrified and scared.

On Tuesday, he looked very sick. We thought that he was bored and hungry. He didn't move around very much. We asked one of the parents, Mrs Carriamis, what we should feed him. She suggested bread. Miss King's father suggested that we put some salt in his water.

On Wednesday, we did as the adults suggested and it worked. Hermit began to scurry around the jar. He looked very lively and happy. He climbed over the shells and around the sides of the jar. He looked like he was trying to get out. We thought that he was lonely and homesick. Maybe he missed his family.

We decided that it was cruel to keep him any longer. We planned to put him into Sydney Harbour when we visited there the next day. Later that afternoon disaster struck! Poor Hermit died. We were very sad.

On Thursday we took Hermit to the Harbour. One of the girls, Lorena, gave him a burial at sea. One of the boys, Patrick, made a speech. He said: "We will remember, with all our hearts, our beloved friend, Hermit."

Certainly Hermit was our friend. We will miss him sadly.

Year 3 Blue (7-8) Our Lady of the Rosary, Kensington

❧ QUICK EMERGENCY! ❧

I was playing in the backyard with my friend Nicole and my dog Shep. Shep was a German Shepherd and loved chasing cats. Nicole and I were trying to teach Shep how to jump over an elastic. We got a rock and tossed it over so he would jump over to catch it but the stupid dog walked around the elastic and picked it up when it had landed.

It is hard to control Shep because we have two cats, Suzy and J-J. Suzy is very old. She is 13. Suzy has only been at-tacked by dogs once. It was a sheep dog who attacked her. He scratched her belly and bit her leg. Suzy hides next door under their house. Around next door's house is a fence with a little hole in it. Suzy fits through the hole but Shep can't so Suzy hides there.

When my brother got home at 6 p.m. I told him that Shep has been getting out the side gate and could he fix it because the pound or someone will get him and maybe even kill him. He told me it was too dark and he would do it tomorrow. In the morning about 9 a.m. I picked up Shep's clean bowl out of the cupboard and filled it up with Meaty Bites and Go-Dog biscuits. When I got out the backyard I called Shep but he wouldn't come. I had a look around the yard but he wasn't there. When I looked at the side gate I saw a huge hole in it where Shep had bitten at it and run away. I dressed myself straight away, hopped on my bike and went looking for him.

I went all around the streets in our neighbourhood but I couldn't find him anywhere, so I came back home and asked Mum would she take me in the car. We went to the R.S.P.C.A. but he wasn't anywhere. I thought we had lost him so we came home.

Just as we were driving up Pearce Avenue, I saw something lying on the ground in one big heap. It started to move a bit so we got out and had a look what it was. Mum and I rolled it over and it was Shep. I screamed NO . . . and started crying. I asked is he dead? "Almost," Mum replied. "We better take him to the vet now and fast."

When we arrived there the vet had a look at him and said, "Very serious. It looks like a truck hit him but I think I can fix him up." That made me feel a lot better. "You can come and pick him up in two days," said the vet. When we arrived home I stomped inside, woke up my brother and said, "Fix the gate NOW! . . . ."

Amanda Ryan (10) Peakhurst PS

ANIMAL STORIES

❧ THE HUNGRY CAT ❧

"Get me some milk," meowed the cat. The boy and the girl got some milk for the cat.

"Get me some meat," meowed the cat. Mum and dad got some meat for the cat.

"Get me some fish," meowed the cat. The girl got some fish for the cat.

"Get me some prawns," meowed the cat. The boy got some prawns for the cat.

"Get me a warm box," meowed the cat, "I want a snooze." Mum got a warm box for the cat.

"At last," said the family. "Let's hope he sleeps for a long time, he is a very hungry cat."

Kindergarten, North Haven PS

❧ THE ITCHY PIG ❧
(A story for Kindergarten)

Oh drat! I'm itchy! All I do all day is scratch! scratch! *scratch!* I can't find a cure and I don't think I will. My owner thinks I am faking — BUT I AM NOT! Oh oink! Oh scratch! Oh itchy-itchy itch!

I make up my mind I won't scratch. What happens the next day?

That's right. S C R A T C H !

I can't find out what causes it — but I better find out soon.

Oh! Oink? Oink? This is terrible.

I know what I'll do. I'll fake sick so the owner will notice. Oh should I?

Itch! Itch! Itch!

Scratch! Scratch! Scratch!

No! If I do I'll end up with a red bottom as well as an itchy tummy!

Oh what can I do? I'll get a good night's sleep and think in the morning.

Oinkkk! Oinkkk! Goink night!

Well, I had a dream last night! It had this Mud Monster coming towards me saying "Roll in me! Roll in me!"

I've got it. (Itch! Itch! Scratch! Scratch!)

I have to have mud. What mud? I don't have any mud! I'll have to look for some.

So off I go singing this song:

"I'm an itchy pig mud-hunter!"

Hello! Hello! What's this?
Mud Glorious Mud!!

So I took myself and fell right in it and rolled and *rolled* and R O L L E D!

It got in my ears and everywhere but it stopped the itch! It just trickled all over me. It was slippery, slimy and soggy. I splashed and S P L A S H E D! It was G L O R I O U S!!

And when I got out of the mud I was brown but itchless. H U R R A Y ! ! !

Joanne Clarke (9) Epping North PS

❧ THE ANIMAL BALL ❧

Once upon a time there lived a famous ballet dancer, her name was Kassandra. One day she heard a knock at the door. She opened the door, there at the door stood a cuddly koala with a postman hat and coat and trousers, he was holding a little letter bag. The koala handed her a little pink envelope, she opened it. The letter read "Ladies in this house are invited to a grand ball." She ticked it and sealed it up and gave it back to the koala. He ran off on his bicycle before he even said goodbye.

At midnight she got ready, for the grand ball was tonight. Suddenly the clock struck 12, bong bong tick bong bong bong bong bong bong bong bong bong.

She ran to the grand ball but when she got there the only people there were all sorts of animals, like dancing kangaroos jumping koalas and wiggling pigs and racing tortoises and slow hares and hopping birds and climbing mouses and opening possums and walking panthers. She ate lots and lots and lots and lots and lots and lots and lots and lots and lots and had some dinner.

Then she danced with different animals and then she ate some more and went home, had a drink and brushed her teeth and went to bed when she had her night clothes on.

Sarah Gerathy (5) Bilgola Plateau PS

❧ THE THREE LITTLE RABBITS ❧

One day three little rabbits were going for a walk. A mean fox saw them and said "Look in my bag to see if there are any holes."

The rabbits looked in the big bag and the fox shut the bag and they heard the fox sharpening the knife. There were some holes in the bag.

One, two, three, the rabbits jumped out of the holes. The fox didn't have any dinner!

Linda Snook (5) Roseville PS

❧ HOW THE RABBIT GOT HIS LONG EARS ❧

Long long ago in the Dreamtime when the land and animals were being made a little rabbit came hopping along the road. He met a cow and the cow said "Do you want some long ears?" and the little rabbit said "Yes, how delightful," and so the cow got a long stick and poked it up his ears and the little rabbit said "Ouch! you hurt me," and the cow said "Sorry." And that's how the rabbits got their long ears.

Clare McNally (6) St Pius X, Unanderra

Once upon a time there were three bears. They lived very happily in a little cottage in the woods.

One morning the mother bear cooked some sandwiches, one each. They had cheese in them. When she took them out they were burning.

So she put them on the table. Then they went for a drive into the city.

When they were gone a little girl came into the cottage. Her name was Kerrie.

She looked at the sandwich and she said to herself, "I do feel a little hungry," so she tasted the biggest sandwich but it was too hot.

So she tried the middle-sized sandwich but it was too cold. Next she tried the baby one and it was yuck, so she went home with nothing to eat!

Kerrie Allott (6) North Albury PS

❧ HOW ECHIDNA GOT HIS QUILLS ❧

"I'm hungry" hissed Python the snake. "So am I" cried Hymi the Native Cat. "I know someone who we can eat and cannot fight" growled Dingo. "Who?" said the others. "Echidna" growled Dingo. Meanwhile Echidna was in the jungle. Then Python, Hymi and Dingo came and they all yelled "I'm hungry" and started chasing Echidna. Echidna ran everywhere but found nowhere to hide so he ran in a green thorny bush. After a while he came out. Echidna had thorns on him and they were stuck. He curled up. Python slithered around Echidna and got hurt. Dingo took a bite. He got hurt. Hymi pounced on Echidna and got hurt. They went away. The ball uncurled and Echidna saw no one around him. The thorns were his quills. He was protected ever after by his sharp quills.

Debbie Crittenden (7) Tuggerawong PS

❧ THE DINGO'S HOWL ❧

Way back in the Dreamtime when animals talked and humans lived in peace, there was a tribe named Kiri Kiri. In the tribe, animals and humans lived together and hunted for food such as grubs, small animals, roots and vegetables. One day they all sat around a big fire and discussed the day's happenings.

Kiechiro, the wisest man of the tribe, was sitting quietly when he overheard a conversation between the Warrigal (Dingo) and the Dinnawan (Emu). The Warrigal, who was a great talker and a large boaster, talked about his day's catches.

"Today I passed the forbidden cave of Youa Ni and I heard a deep groaning sound coming from inside. My curiosity got the better of me and I went in to see what it was. I saw a beautifully coloured bird sitting on a nest. It looked sadly at me, groaned and then closed its eyes. I walked up to it cautiously and realised that it had died. I took its eggs from beneath it and hurried out."

Little did the Warrigal know that he stole the eggs of the great bird Whuhu (the spirit of animals) and that the eggs were going to be its children. Kiechiro knew all about the great spirit Whuhu and shouted out, "The Warrigal has stolen Whuhu's eggs and she shall be avenged. I say we get rid of the Animals before we are destroyed."

But it was too late. Whuhu had summoned a storm to blow through the village and destroy everything in sight. It killed lots of people and mainly animals, but suddenly she halted the storm and said, "I shall spare you all so you can live in peace for all your lives and so may other future generations. But I will punish the animals for the carelessness. They may not be able to talk any more but they shall make noises that may only be understood by their same species. As for the Warrigal he deserves to be dead for his foolishness but I will punish him by making him howl instead of barking so he may not be understood by dogs or his own species."

Ever since then the humans have been in war with animals by killing them and eating them for meat, and the Dingo has always howled.

David Bachali (11) Katoomba PS

NATURE

❧ NIGHT AND DAY ❧

This is a story about the moon and the sun.
The moon and the sun were friends. They used to play.
When it was time to go to bed the sun wanted to keep
a comet.
The moon got angry. He went away and would not see
the sun ever again.
The sun was too hot for the comet. The comet blew up.
The tiny pieces fell to earth. They made the blue mountains.

Todd Bailey, Daniel Keelty, Bradley Mee, Nicholas Chapman,
Samia Rabay, Sandra Mattiazza (6) Holy Spirit, St Clair

Marie Mittiga (10) St Gerard's, Carlingford

❧ CITY LIGHTS ❧

Lady Evening came stepping out of the sky,
As graceful as a swan,
Her dress lined with diamonds,
The clouds, her puffy sleeves,
The moon her gold medallion.
Her husband, Lord Night,
Had aeroplanes embroidered on his cloak,
With a lace hem of fence;
And the black cats on the fence
   Purring and meowing.

The birds fly in the early twilight
Their songs make me happy on wet days.
So happy.
So I like to sing with the birds.
Sing, sing.
No-one can take my music away from me.
Sing, sing.
It's my favourite thing.
If ever anyone takes me away
The birds will still be able to sing.

Peter Parsons (6) Normanhurst West PS

OF WHAT USE ARE WINGS?

Up, up, up,
The kestrel soars,
Through banks of cloud,
The sky's the limit.
Looking over a hooked beak,
Riding on the wind,
Searching.
A checked pattern of clouds are passed over,
Living chessmen busy, working.
Over mountains
Tall and high,
The wind whistling by.
Soon the shape of what is sought,
Although it's small,
Is finally found.
Down, down, down,
The kestrel plummets,
A scream is heard,
A rat is dead.

Lisa Evans (11) Dubbo South PS

PLANTS

A jungle to little creatures,
Inside and out.
Its arms stretch and stretch
With papery hands
Full with veins,
All the legs beneath the ground.

Allan Greer (7) New Lambton PS

AN AUTUMN POEM

The autumn leaves come down
With a sweeping,
swirling,
creeping,
curling,
and a crackling
To the ground.

James Mattinson (6) Normanhurst West PS

WHISPERING WINDS

Whispering wind circled the bare branches,
Carrying summer away on its back
Tunnelling through the leaves
Like a soaring eagle
Pouncing on its prey:
Murdering, seeking revenge.

Polluting the air with frostbitten breezes
Attacking the sun on its run for survival
Its destiny to kill.
Its sentence to fight with spring,
To take over summer.

Stripping the trees,
The ground lays covered in a blanket of sorrow.
Defeated leaves,
Torn by the mean rudiments of winter
Saturated golden brown.
Winter ends.

The good view
I like The view of mount Warning you
geT a very good view up the top. I
Climbed it and mum was lazy.

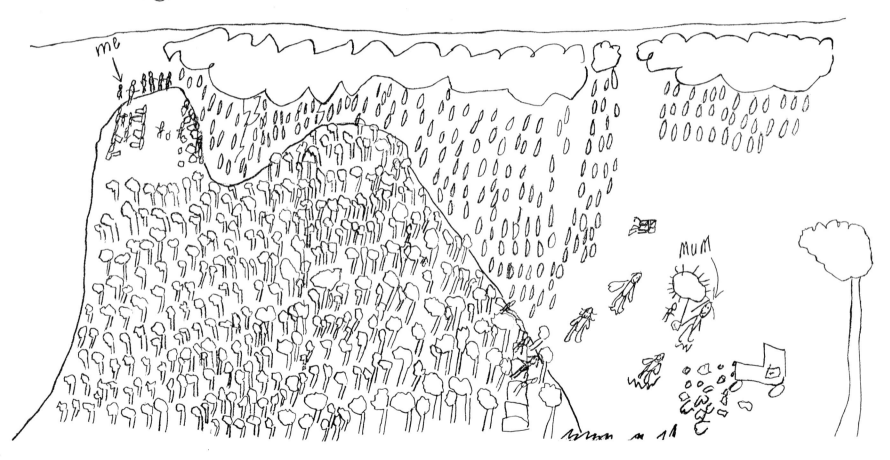

Joel Maycock (6) St Joseph's, Tweed Heads

The wind rests among the clouds
Waiting to rise once again.

Katey McConachy (11) Ourimbah PS

❧ LEAVES ❧

Leaves are fluttering down with
green, red, yellow and brown.
Fluttering with excitement.
Falling into brown rivers and
drifting to the open sea.

Kate Thomas (7) Bankstown West PS

❧ THE OCEAN ❧

The ocean whispers . . . . .
Of cool blowing breezes
Floating softly through the air;
Of moonbeams splashing
Through crystal waves;
Of dolphins somersaulting
Through misty spray;
Of seagulls gliding
Through the pale blue sky;
Of shipwrecks which lie
On the ocean floor;

Of multi-coloured fish
Darting through the coral;
Of golden seaweed
Swaying with the tide;
Of sparkling sand
Swirling silently
Across the ocean floor.

Natalie Manning (11) Abbotsford PS

❧ GREY SHADOW ❧

Silently gliding
Looming menacingly
Grey shark shadow
Mysterious, ominous.

Small fish,
Rainbow coloured
Darting in unison,
This way, that way.
Grey shark shadow!
Small fish
Dashing frantically.
Mangled small fish
Corpses floating.
Savaging shark!

Children swimming
Laughing gleefully
Grey shark shadow!
Shrieking, screaming,
Thrashing water,

41

Confusion reigning,
Many hands reaching.
Ashore, panting painfully,
Safe, gasping.
Man-eating shark!

Gliding away silently
Menacing and threatening
Grey shark shadow
Ominous, destroyer.

Dionne Capanna (10) St Gerard's, Carlingford

≈ WAVES ≈

The waves move in
like soldiers on the march.
Each attacking from the ocean depths
the sand and rocky shore.
They rise, they roar, they rush ahead
line after line comes crashing down
dying on the sand.

S. Magi (11) Mosman C of E Prep

≈ THE LONELY BEACH ≈

As the sun went down,
The windswept beach remained,
Still, quiet.

Nobody came to sit
On its golden sand today,
Nobody.

The wind died down,
The moon was high in the sky.
Every thing was calm.
Peaceful and calm.

Not a word was spoken,
Except for the trees whispering
To one another.
Not a word.

Kylie Duffy (10) St Gerard's, Carlingford

RAIN

The nicest sound
When I go to bed
Is the sound of rain
That I hear instead
Of the silent sound
When the night is clear
Oh how I wish some rain was near.

Melissa Cullen (8)
Melinda Holder (7)
St Philomena's, Moree ▶

Rainy day
And the sky is grey.
I am in bed
Near the window.
Bright colours of the rainbow
Over the trees
Water falling from the sky.
Sun shines through it.

Summer-Brooke Earles (6)
Avondale SDA Primary, Cooranbong

43

CLOUDY PIG

When I look into the sky, I see a pig in the clouds.
It starts to rain and that is the end of that pig.

Chris Osburg (6) Epping Heights PS

I am a raindrop and I want to sit on a cloud. When a parent comes along I am tricky. I slide down their back, then I jump in their shoes. I can get messy.

Becky Barnes (8) John Warby PS, Airds

IMPRISONED BY RAIN

I kneel at my bedroom window looking wistfully out at the misty haze of rain fluttering down constantly from the looming grey clouds above. People's feet can be heard squelching through the few grassless portions of lawn as they walk hurriedly past, flashes of colour seen in the blur. The cold unforgiving wind whistles and rustles the leaves as it goes quickly past and in the dim light the leaves glisten brightly as if they had just been dusted.

Water seems to flood the tarred road and its gutters. As the cars go past a spray comes from beneath their tyres wetting the unaware. There's a splitter splatter to be heard as rain dances lightly on the roofs, then cascades down into gutters for a journey to people's tanks.

The prison gates are still locked as the rains continue endlessly. As for the sun it didn't wink once all day! Today is over now and tomorrow will most probably be fine and sunny. Fingers crossed for freedom!

Rebecca Monk (12) Dubbo South PS

EVENING

I sank thankfully into a worn, tattered, old armchair on our verandah. The day had been as they say, a "scorcher". Old Aboriginal Tabuk, from the neighbouring cattle station, said it would rain today, but he'd been saying that every day for the last two weeks so no-one listened to him any more. I sat and watched the sun setting, the last pale orange streaks of sunlight sifting through the vivid pink clouds. The whole western sky was a mass of colour — yellow, orange, pink, mauve. But then, from the east, a huge, rolling, thundering stormcloud rumbled across the sky. Heavy drops of rain started to fall like the ones that collect on the end of a leaf and somehow manage to find their way down your neck. The wind was next. It sent the pelting rain almost horizontal. It whistled furiously around the tops of tall eucalyptus trees. Soon, the rain decreased to a moderately steady fall. With a sigh, I stood up and slowly made my way to bed.

Katrina Ramsay (11) Mt Pritchard PS

"Floral Cluster" *Eric Hutchens (11) Normanhurst West PS*

◄ "Gum Leaves" *Chau Truong (6) Birchgrove PS*

"Australian Animals"   *Class 2G (7-8) St Edward's, Tamworth*

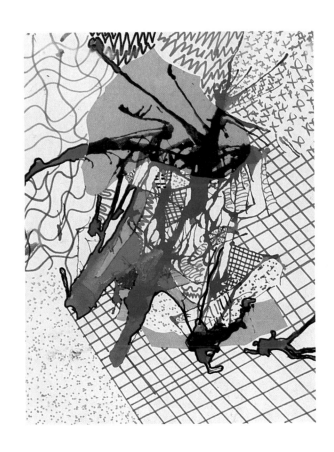

Class 4-1 (9-10) Ascham, Edgecliff

◄   *Nazih Kabbara (10) Earlwood PS*

Roderick Kumar (10) St Patrick's, Asquith

Paul Cochrane (10) St Patrick's, Asquith

FIRE

🌿 FIRE 🌿

Greyish red
Crackle and sizzle
Like coloured pointy teeth
I like fire
It is warm.

Yanni Kronenberg (5) Australia St Infants, Newtown

🌿 FIREWORKS 🌿

Fireworks explode with a bang.
Fireworks crash on the ground.
Fireworks light up the clouds.
Kaboom kaboom! Kapow kapow!
Fireworks whizzing, fireworks fizzing.
Fireworks swirling, fireworks twirling.
Look at the sparkles fall from the sky.
Look at the flames booming and zooming.
Sizzling like a sausage
Floating in the air.
Twirling swirling Fizzing whizzing
Booming zooming Bang bang
B A N G !

Elizabeth King (7) Woolgoolga PS

Today we saw the firefighters at school. We could go in the fire engine. We saw oxygen in the fire engine. There were three walkie-talkies. There were three hoses on the top. Mothers came to watch. Then we went into the library. The firefighters showed us their uniform. They said how to get people out when they are trapped.

Marija Mravunac (6) Maroubra Junction PS

🌿 THE RED DEATH 🌿

In the dry outback a little homestead stood. The heat wilted the flowers on the window ledge. A gust of wind came and with it a little spark. Down it comes on a dry leaf. The little spark was soon a small fire. The fire soon spreads and grows. Giant flamey fingers jumping up, and when the fire is out there is nothing left.

Michelle Staples (7) Modanville PS, via Lismore

🌿 THE FIRE 🌿

A few weeks ago I was playing in my bedroom. It was just before lunch. I could hear the birds in the trees outside. The sound of the waves beyond the bush made me feel cool.

I smelt smoke outside. I had a look out my bedroom window. I saw flames in the distance. They were big orange flames jumping from the ground to the trees. The fire was moving fast because the wind was blowing hard. I got so frightened because it was so big and hot that I nearly forgot to call my Mum and Dad. It kept coming out of the trees in giant puffs of black smoke.

I said, "Yes, I have time to ring the Fire Brigade." I ran to the telephone. They said they would come right away.

The next thing to do was to call Mum and Dad. As soon as they answered me I said "Run!" They wondered why. Then they smelt it too. They called back to me and said, "Save as much as you can." I stuffed some clothes and some photos into a garbage bag and I ran to the beach.

I got out pretty quickly but my Mum and Dad took longer. I looked out for them but I could not see them. I wondered where I was going to sleep the night and what I was to have for breakfast the next day.

Then I saw a grass patch with plants around it. I said, "That will do me." I ran over to the grass patch and watched the fire come closer. They were still orange flames, but they were a lot bigger and there were a few sparks of red with some bright yellow mixed in. I could smell the unpleasant, dirty smell of the smoke. It made me choke and splutter. I started to feel hot and the perspiration kept trickling down my body.

I felt terribly frightened and with all the exhaustion of my fear I fell asleep.

The sun went down and the moon came up.

Then it was morning. I felt the morning sun warming me. I looked around to see if my Mum and Dad were anywhere around. They weren't. Then I decided to go and have a look at the house.

When I got there the house and my Mum and Dad had disappeared in a tumble of black timber.

I felt black inside, too.

Sharlene Ripamonti (8) Concord West PS

46

❧ BUSHFIRE ❧

The angry flames are burning,
The sparks are flying around,
There's crackling and there's churning,
Black ashes on the ground.

Smell the charcoal burning black,
Animals flee along the track,
The flames are yellow, orange, red,
All the trees are nearly dead,
Where the fresh forest used to grow,
Now there's nothing left to show.

Carey Jackson (10) Kororo PS

❧ HOT STUFF ❧

. . . As every man and his wife fled the township of Bushtown, one man stood guarding his house, this was his pride and joy. No bushfire had ever been able to break this proud old man, but this one seemed destined to. As the fire raged down the dry gulley, the old man vigorously pumped water into his pipe. On all sides the fire cracked and destroyed, but the old man still stood tall. As the fire came closer the old man's heart began to thump hard against his weak skin, feeling as though it would burst any minute.

There had been a devastating drought for the last four months and everything was as dry as a bone. This fact didn't help a bit. A harsh wind was blowing and flames often jumped past the man only to be stamped out by the hard sole of the man's boot. The heat was so intense that half the water ended up on the old man's weary body, cooling him down.

Soon he tired, he struggled to stop the fire. Then one flame passed him, this time no hard sole came stamping down and the flame became a raging fire surrounding the man and his house. The intense heat of the flames scorched the man. As his house caught on fire and slowly collapsed, so did the old man and like the house, he never rose again.

James Solomon (11) Newport PS

❧ JUST A NEIGHBOUR ❧

Her face looked so sad. From where I was standing, even her profile looked sad. Her mouth drooped and no longer had that chirpy smile. Her eyes hung and were brimming with tears. She looked like she would cry any minute. Slowly the tears fell. She made no sound but tears continued to fall. Faster and faster they came. Suddenly, she let out a low moan. She kept moaning and crying. Then she fell to the ground and started to weep. I wanted to go over and comfort her but my legs wouldn't let me. So I just stood there quietly, watching.

Her house, well what used to be her house was now nothing but ashes and memories. You could actually smell the burning and death in the air. The girl was at a music lesson when it happened. Her mother, father and brother were at home. When she got home her house was still burning. There were fire engines, police cars and trucks. But most of all, there was fire. Flames quivering. Heat rushing out into the open air. Heatwaves. Smelling like, well burnt. Very burnt. One touch would sizzle your finger slowly and painfully. Like it did the house.

My ears could hear, "Help me, help me!" like the house crying out in pain. I wanted to save it. We all wanted to save it. But we couldn't. It felt like a volcano about to erupt inside me. Like a balloon that has just burst. Then, all of a sudden, the heat, the flames, the burning smell all died down. All that is left is a black empty hole. Black ashes scatter to the ground but the strong wind sends them up in a whirl and then blows them away.

The girl is waiting. Waiting for someone to take her away from this horrible sight. An aunt, an uncle, a grandmother. What do I know? I am just a neighbour.

Her mother is dead. Her father and brother are dead. All her possessions are lost. Everything she owns, gone.

Her tears are dry now and her face streaked with dirt. A stick falls in my direction. It makes a loud 'crunch'. She does not notice.

A blue Datsun pulls up in front of this depressing scene. A middle-aged woman steps out and puts her arm around the girl. She is sobbing. Slowly she climbs into the car. Without warning, her eyes meet mine. Those sad, confused, begging eyes. She turns away. Wanting to run to her, to comfort her, but of course, my feet won't let me.

The motor starts up. The car begins to pull away. She does not even glance my way. Who was that woman anyway? Is the girl going to live with her? If so, where is the house?

But then again, what do I know? I am just a neighbour.

Nicole Sandler (11) Masada College, St Ives

47

AUSTRALIAN IMAGES

❧ TRANSPORTATION TO NEW SOUTH WALES ❧

I'm a starving waif and my face is paler than the colour white. I have spindly legs and I am unwanted and unloved. The grimy hands I have are as brown as brown could be. My hair is knotted and very untidy. I am bruised, dull and lifeless. My clothes are ragged and dirty. My name is Katherine Pearce and I am ten years old.

I was sitting on an old, cobblestone street when a lady came across the road carrying a basket full of fruit. I thought she wouldn't mind me taking a piece. So I crept up behind her but I tripped over a piece of cobblestone. She saw me and called over a burly policeman who took me to gaol.

I was in a dark, smelly cell for three days before I came before the magistrate. I trembled and shook when he said I had to go to a strange place called New South Wales.

We boarded a ship which had a room at the bottom for us convicts. It was a very rough trip which took eight months for us to get to New South Wales.

When we arrived at our destination I was sent to work as a housemaid for one of the officers. They treated me well and then I knew that New South Wales wasn't that bad and my lot was sure to change.

Katherine Pearce (10) Baulkham Hills North PS

❧ THE EXPLORER ❧

Slowly
He drags his horse
Through the endless heat
Of the desert.

Fame,
That's what he desires.
Others suffer —
He doesn't care.

Pale and forlorn
From hunger and thirst
The horse dies
Slowly and painfully.

He is lost,
No-one cares.
Now he deserves
What he gets.

Lyn Kimson (11) John Purchase PS, Cherrybrook

❧ KANGAROO ❧

Russet red long tailed balancer
Powerful hind legs
Alert and fleet
Bounding across the plain.

Justin Graham (9) Thornleigh West PS

🐦 THE KOOKABURRA 🐦

He sat in his tree
And he knew he was free
No cages, no bars for him.

His life was his own
And he lived it alone
Sitting with a smile, on his limb.

Not a creature did scare him
Not an animal dared him —
To a fight he would surely win.
No one complained that he was insane
Because of the din he made.

He feasted on snakes
Drank water from lakes
And lived his life alone —
Lived his life on his own.

Kristen Bobak (11) Padstow North PS

🐦 THE DROVER AND HIS WIFE 🐦

What a life
Has the drover's wife!
Left all alone
While her husband is gone
Driving cattle
And having to battle
Flooding streams
And horrible dreams!

Her dog, Alligator
A vicious tormentor
Protects her from snakes
And many other fates
He hunts for his food —
A dead kangaroo,
Or a grass snake, might
Be his dinner tonight.

Her name is Victoria Lee
A scruffy, worn woman is she
A woman gentle and kind
She has an interesting mind
She never ever cries
But often wonders why
Her husband takes so long to come back
To their old, rambling, paperbark shack.

Ruth Yallop (9) Epping North PS

❧ ANZACS ❧

We sat down in our trenches,
Our slouch hats on our head.
We had worn uniform proudly
From the beginning as they'd said.

The Turks looked down upon us
From the safety of the hill.
The guns pointing at us,
Waiting for the kill.

We sat down in the trenches.
We didn't have a chance.
We sat down in the trenches,
Till they told us to advance.

Sarah Purchase (10) Turramurra North PS

❧ A STORY ABOUT ANZAC DAY ❧

Anzac Day commemorates the landing of the Australian and New Zealand troops at Gallipoli on the 25th April, 1915. This day is a public holiday in Australia and New Zealand in honour of all those who lost their lives serving the two countries in the two world wars. A large number of Australian children enjoy this holiday, but do not know who the first Anzacs really were. The word ANZAC was first used when a combined corps of Australian and New Zealand forces was set up in 1914 under Lord Kitchener. The two commanders of the Australian and New Zealand troops asked if they could be called the Australian and New Zealand Army Corps. This was shortened to ANZAC.

The name Anzac has always been important to me because my pa's name is Thomas Anzac McSeveny. He was called Thomas Anzac because he was born on the 24th March, 1916, on the day his brother, Jimmy, came home from the army with a medical discharge.

I would like to now tell you the story of a very brave Anzac who was one of the bravest of our soldiers at Gallipoli.

His name was John Simpson Kirkpatrick although he was also called John Simpson but was better known as 'the man with the donkey'. Private Simpson landed on Gallipoli at dawn on 25th April, 1915. He was a member of the 3rd Field Ambulance Australian Army Medical Corps. That night he found a donkey in one of the gullies and intended to use him to carry soldiers who suffered leg wounds. He called this donkey Duffy. Each day and half of every night he and his donkey worked endlessly to carry water up the steep gully to the fighting for the wounded soldiers. Then back they came with a badly hurt soldier on Duffy's back.

Every trip he faced deadly ambushes and fierce shrapnel fire but this never stopped him. He risked his life many times to save others on the battle field. He was always cheerful and caring to the wounded soldiers. He was like "The Good Samaritan" and every one admired his courage and bravery. The Indian soldiers called him "Bahadar". This meant "the bravest of the brave".

For twenty three days Private Simpson and his donkey worked to help save other lives but on the 19th of May he was shot through the heart while bringing back a badly hurt soldier on Duffy's back. He had saved many lives at the cost of his own. He was recommended for a bravery sword but didn't receive one.

Simpson and his donkey became a legend and remind us of all the unselfish and heroic deeds at Gallipoli. Private Simpson showed us that even in the horror of war he was able to help and care for his mates, even though he himself was killed.

Ben McSeveny (10) Faulconbridge PS

❧ SIR DOUGLAS MAWSON'S JOURNAL 1907 ❧

Wednesday 10th June
Day one. A lot colder than I expected. Light blizzard starting. Husky dogs very active.

Thursday 11th June
Light blizzard has turned into a bad blizzard and forced us to stay inside our tents for ten days. I have realised Mertz is a very good chess player.

Sunday 21st June
Still cold but blizzard has stopped. Dogs getting tired from walking through the snow. Ninnis is becoming a real pain in the neck. He is making funny faces and pulling our goggles tight and then letting go of them.

Monday 22nd June
Ninnis is behaving now. Dogs are getting weak because they ran at the start of our journey. Our food supply is getting low.

Tuesday 23rd June
Another blizzard starting. This time not as bad. Only in tent six days and I have vowed never to play chess with Mertz again.

Monday 29th June
Food supply getting lower. We have to turn back. Travelling for a while, nothing has really happened. Suddenly, we came to a crevasse. Ninnis fell in and died. And worse yet, he had the sled with most of our food.

Tuesday 30th June
Still sad about Ninnis. We travel on. I think a blizzard is starting. Fortunately, we were wrong. Food is very low.

Wednesday 1st July
Long way to go. Still going through snow with low food supply. Have to kill dogs to eat.

Thursday 2nd July
Eating dogs has poisoned us. Painful to walk. Mertz is very sick, so sick that he has collapsed. I carried him until he died. I am alone now with not much food and a bad blizzard starting.

Friday 3rd July
Bad blizzard has forced me to stay in the tent for a couple of days, at least Mertz isn't here to beat me at chess.

Sunday 12th July
Started off again, but before I left I cut the sled in half and put what food I had left on one half. I travelled on.

Monday 13th July
Weak and sick, I journeyed through the snow. As I approached a crevasse and walked across the ice bridge, it broke and I fell in. But the rope I pulled the sled with broke my fall. Because of the sickness caused by eating the dogs, my skin was coming off in large chunks and it was painful to climb but I had to. When I reached the top, I continued my journey.

Tuesday 14th July
Shocked by what happened yesterday and delayed by another blizzard, I stayed in my tent for several days. I am very weak and hungry.

Wednesday 22nd July
Blizzard has cleared up completely. I travel on. Ahead I see a bag of food. As soon as I reach it I read the note on it. It says there is a cave ahead.

Thursday 23rd July
When I reached the cave I went in. There was a blanket and more food. I waited there for about a week until the search party arrived and took me back home.

John Bain (9) Sacred Heart, Kooringal

NO SNOW AT CHRISTMAS

No snow at Christmas
In this sunburnt land.
Shearing starts again,
Flies hang round a daggy ewe
Givin' her a temper —
That's all!

The dogs are barking,
Pudding cooking,
Horses resting after work.
Drought is coming
For all I know.

Stars in the sky,
Trees on the ground,
Moon has risen
And is surveying all.
All there is to say —
Merry Christmas!

Michelle O'Neill (12) St Patrick's, Cooma

THE SURFING EASTER BUNNY

One night it was Easter. I knew the easter bunny was coming so I stayed up until 12 o'clock. He didn't come, so finally I went to sleep.

You'll never guess why he was late. He was riding the waves at One Mile and they were twenty five feet high! Luckily he'd left all the eggs in an esky on the sand.

At last he arrived at my house. He tried to sneak in but I heard him arrive at 6 o'clock. His fluffy ears were soaking wet, and dripping down his light blue singlet. His white sandy tail popped out of his okanuis, and his nose was burnt and peeling. He was a mess! He gave me a chocolate easter bunny that didn't look a bit like him. It was normal.

Luke Anderson (8) Forster PS

AUSTRALIA

Australia is the cork hats,
The zinc cream and the pies,
The Fosters and the damper,
The T-shirts and the flies.

The wombat and the wallaby,
The brolga and the snake,
The vegemite and the mossie bite
And big Australian steak.

MMMMMmmmmmmmmm!

Trisha Delofski (11) Abbotsford PS

THE AVERAGE DAY OF A TRUE BLUE AUSSIE

G'day. The name's Kimberley, but all me mates just call me Kim. I'm the fair dinkum example of a true blue Aussie koala. I'm gunna tell you 'bout the most average sort of day in the life of the most average sort of koala — me.

The day got off to a lousy start at flaming 4 a.m. when the rowdy kookas started screaming.

"Struth," I thought. "Can't they give a fella a decent rest?" I felt like climbing up the tree and telling them what I thought of them but I was too blooming whacked. I did decide to get meself some brekky. Unfortunately for me though, the bleeding tree branch that I was standing on snapped and I shot down the tree at about 100 k's an hour. When I landed I wasn't too sore, but the goanna that I landed on was a bit shaken up. As he crawled away I caught sight of me mate Bluey the kanga.

"Stone the crows Kim, great fall," he said. " I thought you were a goner."

"Yeah. Stroke of luck that Bill was in the way."

"I reckon. You wanna come down to the pub an' drink it off?"

"Well . . . I dunno. I did say to me mum that I'd cut down on the grog . . ."

"Mabel's gunna be there."

"Let's go."

Mabel's me girlfriend. She's a bit thick but y'know it's not too good for a bloke t'have a sheila who's got more up top than he has.

So, anyway, we went to the pub and got into the light amber fluid. After that, Mabel, Bluey, some of me other mates and me went down the bush track and had a barbie — and a few more tinnies. It was a good night and what with one thing and another I didn't make it home till after 3.

After a lot of mucking round I finally hit the sack, then about five minutes later, wouldn'cha know it, the flaming galoots in the tree next door started their screaming again. And so another day started — but that's another yarn.

Kate Rowe (11) Forest Lodge PS

🐛 🐛 🐛

FUN

❧ PARTY TIME ❧

Giving a party can be great
It's alright if you don't arrive late
Dinner for two
Special for you
Breakfast and brunch
Dinner and lunch
Awkward guests
Are such pests
Cocktail time
Drinks with lime
Buffet style
Wait for a while.

Jessica Lopez (7) Faulconbridge PS

Slibberly, slobberly, slop,
My mum uses a vacuum mop.
She mops up all the Gibilygoo,
So the carpet looks like new.
The Gibilygoo are funny critters,
They're nearly the same as Mulydippers.
They eat the carpet all day long,
Then they sing a Shillershock song.
The sound they make makes ears go buzz,
Like a giant Millyfuzz.
And that's why my mum has a vacuum mop.
Slibberly, slobberly, slop.

Leonie Messner (11) Yates Avenue PS, Dundas

❧ THE YETI ❧

The Yeti is a jigo beast
With cluthing claws and fangled feet,
He rambles up the mountain side
"We're afraid of him" the people cried.

They watch him golish through the snow
On his three big feet and one big stow,
Into his cave and out of sight
With his drumknok florking and his Gistle white.

Terror of night and terror of day
Till trapped by the Munchmins in the middle of May,
Scrawled from his cave and hacked with a zif
An' now Yeti lies all drold and stiff.

Toby Cremer (11) Killara PS

❧ MOG'S STORY ABOUT C ❧

Mog is a cat.
He drives a car.
His pet is a crocodile.
He gets milk from a cow.
He drinks from a cup.
He eats from a can.

He rides a camel.
He sleeps in a cradle.
He wears a cap.

He walks like a crab.
Mog is crazy.

Mickey Kelly (5) St Brigid's, Gwynneville

54

Mrs Jemima Jakes from Binnaburra
Was the proud owner of a kookaburra,
Which sat on the table and drank hot tea,
With table manners polite as can be.

The kookaburra's name was Jacko Dear,
He had an absolutely terrific ear
For hearing things uncivil and rude,
No wonder the postman said he was crude!

Now, Mrs Jakes was a Christian woman
And NEVER would say words such as "bloomin",
But this kookaburra spoke with words uncouth,
When angered, he was known to screech "Strewth!"

One election day Mrs Jakes went to vote,
On her pink ballot slip she wrote
"I want Edwina Jolly to win,
So don't you dare put my form in the bin!"

When all the votes had been tallied,
The people of the town were loudly rallied.
The honourable winner was declared:
Mr William James Tickleby-Baird!

"It isn't fair!" Mrs Jakes did cry,
"I'm so disgusted I could die!"
But then she thought of a brilliant scheme
And her lively eyes began to gleam.

Mrs Jakes leapt to her feet
While to the floor crashed her seat!
"Fellow citizens, let us celebrate
With our new mayor, this important date!"

When they heard this, the townspeople cheered!
And so for the next week, a banquet was geared.
The town wanted to show off their magnificent new mayor
To the Press, the Premier, and whoever was there.

In the town hall, laden tables groaned
Beneath the weight of the feast. A voice intoned
"Ladies and Gentlemen, rise for your Mayor."
In strutted the celebrity, his nose in the air.

The banquet began. Soup was first course.
The Mayor slurped it noisily and sprayed it with force
Onto his neighbours, then licked his knife clean
While ranting at the Premier, Mr Hygiene.

The Mayor gnawed his bones, as clean as a dog,
And gobbled his food, like Ma Riley's hog.
"Strewth! What a pig!" yelled Jacko Dear,
As down the Mayor's shirtfront dribbled his beer.

By now, the townspeople were feeling unsure,
Was he the right Mayor? Should they show him the door?
The new mayor, however, noticed nothing of the sort,
And continued to belch, to crunch and to snort.

Screeched Jacko: "Blimey! Will you look at that!"
As the Mayor licked his plate; no wonder he's fat!
"I'm disgusted!" cried the butcher, Mr Mackay,
"I've seen better manners in a pig sty!

Are you really our Mayor? You'll never be mine!"
Chorused the town, "You MUST resign!
We'll have Edwina Jolly for Mayor.
She's our choice — she's fair and square!"

"Aha, Jacko! T'was a marvellous plan!"
Crowed Mrs Jakes. "We're rid of that man!
Let's go back home and have some tea.
You've much better manners than ever had he!"

Miranda Nagy (11) Figtree PS

❧ JOHNNIE CAKES ❧

Ingredients:

3 cups self raising flour
3 teaspoons salt
3 ozs (90 grams) butter
1/2 cup milk
1/2 cup water

Utensils:

electric frypan
mixing bowl
knife
egg flipper
flour sifter
wooden board

Method:

Step 1. Sift flour and salt into bowl (don't drop it everywhere). Rub in butter with your clean hands, of course, till the mix resembles fine even breadcrumbs.

Step 2. Make a well in the centre, don't fall in. Add mix of milk and water all at once, try not to drown. Stir with sharp knife using cutting motion. (Cut your fingers and you'll spoil it).

Step 3. Turn onto floured surface, knead lightly but don't lose your temper and go mad.

Step 4. Roll into flat little balls but don't get out of hand. Flatten on the frypan. They'll cook in a minute so be patient. Shove it into the golden syrup, honey or jam. (Don't stuff yourself).

Result:

They turn out crisp and yummy. Wait for them to cool off before you eat them otherwise you'll burn your tongue. Then you'll know it.
     Have a good time eating it!

Melissa de Silva (11) Carlton PS, Bexley

❧ From DANIEL'S ACTIVITY BOOK ❧

Get a hard boiled egg and some wax crayons.
Draw patterns on the egg and put it in some coloured dye.
Take the egg out after 5 minutes. It should look good.

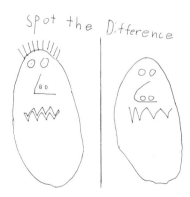

Daniel Hodgson (7) St Anthony's, Wanniassa

TALL TALES

❧ KATRINA'S DISAPPEARING WALKER ❧

My walker disappeared today.
I could not find it.
Michael said it has walked away by itself.
I looked outside.
Michael looked up in the sky and there it was.
It was flying over Michael's home.
Michael put on his Superman's cape and he flew up and got it.
I laughed, Michael laughed.
I took my walker home.

Katrina Leayr (7) & Michael Sheriff (5) Stuart SSP, Valentine

Hi my name is Debra, I live on a farm and I have 20 pigs. One day my daddy went down to the pig shop and bought a pig. He brought it home and put it in the pen. Daddy saw the pig fly backwards. He ran out the back and caught it and took it back to the shop. I laughed and laughed because I had never seen a pig fly backwards. He told the shop keeper that he saw the pig fly backwards. Well, he came back very very angry because the man at the shop would not give his money back. He said pigs can not fly at all so how would one fly backwards.

Debra Burgess (7) Cessnock West PS

❧ From WHEN I WAS FOUR ❧

One morning when I was looking for some mice in the cupboard I found a lot of things you need for cooking. I caught a mouse and put him in the frypan. Then I put him on the stove. I had put the stove on too high and it shrivelled. I had to scrub and scrub and scrub so the food wouldn't taste like you were eating a mouse. Then I found some food you do eat. I had carrots, milk, potatoes, cabbage, zucchinis, biscuits and tomatoes. When I found all that I put it in the frypan. I put some pepper and salt on the food. Then I remembered about the mince so I got it and tipped it in. I had the pan on so high it cooked very, very quickly. I tasted it. It was delicious. I yelled to Mum. "Come in here for a minute please." She walked in. I showed her what I had cooked. I said, "Taste it." She tasted it and she said it was very, very, very nice. I wrote down all the things I used and the method on a piece of paper and put it in the recipe book.

Angus Kingston (10) Lowesdale PS

❧ THE PTERODACTYL AND ME ❧

One night, when I was in bed, a Pterodactyl came into my bedroom. It did a power dive at me. I grabbed its tail and pushed it up. It hit the fan and stayed there. It stayed there all night.

In the morning, my mum and dad woke me up. They saw the Pterodactyl up on the fan. They said, "What's that Pterodactyl doing on the fan?" They ran outside and grabbed a stick and hit it off the fan.

The next day we took it to the Museum. Everyone stared at it. They couldn't believe it was true.

Nathan Pearce (5) Rose Bay PS

❧ THE ANIMAL ADVENTURE ❧

One day when I was going to play with my soccer ball, I saw a polar bear in my back yard. It was white with a black nose and claws as sharp as a forty foot knife. "He will be my pet," I thought. "Until Mum kicks him out." I said, "Do you want to play soccer?" But he said, "Grrrrrrrrr." I ran inside.

Patrick Heads (7) St Mary's, Tenambit

❧ THE DAY I MET AN ORANGE MONSTER ❧

Once upon a time there was a gigantic orange tree. One day I went to pick one of the oranges but just as I picked it, out jumped a big hairy, scary Monster. He growled at me but after a while we became friends. He was a very kind and loving hairy Monster. It's just that he'd been lonely for a long while. That's why he was scary at the first time. It was fun taking him for show and tell day. It was also fun riding on his back. It was also fun snuggling up in his nice warm hairy hair at winter. He had red eyes and a big black shiny nose. But a few weeks later my mum and dad said that I had to take him back to the orange tree where he belonged. After a while he liked living back under the orange tree but we still meet him now and then.

Joseph Russell (8) Canowindra PS

❧ THE DINOSAUR ADVENTURE ❧

One day I awoke and there was Something in my room. I looked in my Dinosaur books and I found out it was a Triceratops. All the Dinosaurs came back to life. A Diplodocus had its head in my window. When I got to school Dinosaurs were everywhere. A Stegosaurus was in my class room. When I got home that day milk, cheese, and half-eaten biscuits were everywhere because a Pterodactyl, Tyrannosaurus Rex and a Woolly Mammoth had been in the cupboards. A Duck-billed Dinosaur was jumping on my bed. One day I made a drink for the Dinosaurs and it made them shrink so I used them as toys that don't need batteries to move.

Michael Taylor (7) Holy Innocents, Croydon

❧ THE UNUSUAL PILL ❧

When I was two I wanted to be a doctor so when mummy was not looking I sneaked an unusual pill. When I swallowed it suddenly I shrank and all my clothes fell on top of me. So I wrapped some paper around me and I dived off the stool. Luckily I landed in my dog's drinking bowl. I jumped into my matchbox car and drove off the steps, got out and got some string (it looked like rope to me) and flung it up to the table. I climbed up. I tried to pick up a pen but it was too heavy. Just as I was about to give up I saw a pill on the kitchen table. I thought it could not do any more harm so I had a nibble and I grew back to my normal size. I put my clothes on just as my mum walked in.

Haydn Miller (7) Bilgola Plateau PS

HOW PAUL'S EARS GREW

Once upon a time Paul was playing with his toy dog on the floor. He loved his toy dog. Every day when he came home from school, he played with it until it broke. Paul cried and cried. His mother came in and said, "Why are you crying?" He said, "My toy dog is broken."

His mother said, "You can glue it." Paul put it together. There was a drop of glue on the table. Paul heard a noise, it went "Tweet". It came from the table. He put his ears on the table to find out what it was. He tried to take them off. He pulled and pulled trying to get his ears unstuck. Paul's ears began to grow. He pulled so hard his ear was not stuck on the table. His ears were so long when he went down the street everyone laughed at Paul.

Peter Dunn (8) Griffith East PS

THE BIGGEST GIANT IN THE WHOLE WORLD

A long, long time ago lived a giant called Humpbuck. He was the BIGGEST GIANT IN THE WORLD. He had enormous eyes, ears, feet, toes, arms and fingers. But there was something that made Humpbuck's life very difficult for him.

As he was really very big and had a big body, Humpbuck had an enormous appetite. But he only had the tiniest mouth in the universe. So he couldn't eat much very quickly.

His wife cooked him only spaghetti so that he could suck it up through the little hole in his huge face. When Humpbuck sucked up the spaghetti he went cross-eyed and red in the face. Before long Humpbuck grew sick and tired of sucking up spaghetti.

After his tea one night he went into his great big bedroom. He squashed an enormous little finger into his tiny mouth. He pushed and shoved. His finger slipped in. He pulled and tugged and pulled and tugged. He did this for an hour or more. He was exhausted.

59

At last he fell off his chair with a thud. He looked into the mirror and saw there a big mouth. It was the size of a merry-go-round. AND THAT'S BIG!

He told his wife and she was surprised. Then he started eating all sorts of foods. When he ate spaghetti he remembered his small mouth.

Jane Kearins (8) St Mary's, West Wyalong

❧ MONSTER MUNCH ❧

Once upon a time there lived a monster. One day he was very, VERY hungry. He went plodding down the road. Then he came to a castle. Then he roared, "Oh, lovely. I love castles!" There came a cry from high up, "Don't eat me!"

The monster took fright, turned the other way and ran as fast as he could. The noise was deafening and the earth shook. All the houses bounced up and down off the earth. He ran around the world for two years, until he ran off the side of the world.

But, then, he found himself floating around in space. He landed on Halley's comet and, if he is still there, he might fall into the sea and get swallowed by a sea serpent.

Claire Baker (8) Gunnedah PS

❧ THE SHOOTING STAR ❧

One night when I was getting into bed I saw a shooting star. It shone into my room.

I looked out of my telescope. It looked beautiful.

The next night I saw another shooting star.

In the morning I went outside. I saw the shooting star lying on the ground. I picked it up. It talked to me. I was amazed.

It said, "Take me to the pond please." So I took him to the pond. The shooting star jumped out of my hand and had a drink.

I took my shooting star to school. All the children wanted a hold. I let all my best friends have a hold. But the shooting star kept jumping back into my hands.

When I got home I called my shooting star Sparkle. The next morning the shooting star was dead. I was very sad.

Melissa Sheehy (7) Kyogle PS

❧ MACHINITIS ❧

One cheerful Sunday morning
I heard a knock at the door,
When I went along to open it,
You won't believe what I saw!

I saw a kind of person
(That's what I think he was)
He may have been an alien
From the planet Zobotroz.

His body was all silver,
His hair a metal gold,
He had a very wrinkled face,
I think he was rather old.

In his hand he held a sign,
"Ban machines" it simply said,
He smiled at me and waved his hand,
I backed away instead.

Class 3-1 (8-9) Ascham, Edgecliff

"The witch threatens Rapunzel's father because he is stealing her lettuce"
Rachel Clegg (7) Roseville PS

From "Charlie and the Chocolate Factory"
Leah Vos (7) St Mary's, Milton

"Hello there, mate," he said,
"I come from year 3444,
We were overrun by machines,
I couldn't cope any more!

They won't do jobs at all,
Instead they rule over us,
Robots, you know, and computers,
All that kind of stuff.

So my friends and I got together
And painted our bodies and hair,
We wanted to look like machines
So we wouldn't get treated unfair."

"Hey wait!" I cried angrily,
"You've got it all so wrong!
Machines are as important
As bats in the game ping-pong!

We've flown around the world
And gone to visit the moon,
Why, we'll even be visiting
Other planets and galaxies soon!"

I listed all the machines
That we use around the home,
TVs, cars and radios,
Toasters and the telephone.

"You're right," said the person,
"Machines are good!" and then
He suddenly disappeared,
And all was normal again.

That night I lay in bed and thought
Of all the machines I'd listed,
I heard my watch beep nine times
And was glad machines existed!

Helen Chisholm (9) Lindfield PS

❧ THE DAY THE HOOVER WENT MAD ❧

One winter's day Mrs Milly Mouldy decided to have a clean-up day. A clean-up day was definitely needed. Dust was on top of the piano, book shelves, TV set, sideboard and most other places where dust tends to gather. There were biscuit crumbs trodden into the carpet. The kitchen table was sticky. In fact, the whole place looked like a rat's nest. Out came brooms, dusters, detergent, three aprons for Mrs Milly Mouldy and the old Hoover vacuum cleaner. She plugged in the vacuum cleaner and went to work picking up the magazines and what-not that were littering the floor. Mrs Milly Mouldy was just picking up a 1978 edition of Time magazine, when the vacuum cleaner sprang to life and started whizzing around the room. Mrs M. M. grabbed hold of the handle, hoping to stop the mad thing but it just kept going round and round the room, causing havoc wherever it went. The cat yowled as the Hoover tried to suck it up, tail first!

Then something amazing happened. The plug flew out of the power point but to Mrs Milly Mouldy's suprise, the vacuum cleaner stopped long enough to throw her onto the bean bag before speeding out the door at 200 km/hour. Pretty soon the bag burst and biscuit crumbs, bird seed and other grot went flying every which way. Instead of going into the bag, all the dirt spattered cars and trees, not to mention people. The Hoover, which was now halfway across Pennant Hills Road, suddenly stopped and smoke started rising from the horrible thing. Mrs Milly Mouldy, who had followed her vacuum cleaner out, watched with relief as a truck approached. Crunch! That was the end of the old Hoover vacuum cleaner.

Lisa Holman (11) Normanhurst West PS

❧ MY WILD BIKE RIDE ❧

I'd just joined this cool bike gang. Cockroach, the chief, told me that I had to do something cool first. I was a bit nervous but of course I agreed.

Next day I was rummaging through the old chicken shed at the back of the paddock. When I say old, I mean old! Something big and bulky was under an old blanket. I pulled it off and stared at what lay underneath. I couldn't believe my eyes! I was staring at a Penny Farthing bike my size!

Quickly I figured Cockroach and the gang would be impressed if I took this bike along and rode it down St. Mary's Drive. (I didn't stop to think about brakes.)

Meeting day was Tuesday. I rode along ten minutes early. I jumped off my bike and grazed my knee. "Great start!" I told myself.

Soon Spider, Slug, Tawny, Spike and Cockroach arrived wearing their black leather jackets and cool sunglasses.

"Where'd ya getta hold of this baby?" asked Spike kicking the handlebars.

"Yea! Where'd you get it kiddo?" Slug demanded.

"Fellas, say nothing and watch this," I smirked, a big grin on my face. I pulled up my sleeves and ran my hand through my hair.

Pedalling down St. Mary's Drive was a cinch (or so I thought). Cruising as fast as possible down the steep hill was a

bit scary but I didn't let it show. Suddenly the fact hit my brain I had no brakes.

Five metres away was a huge brick wall. I felt like dying. Four metres, three metres, two metres and blast off! I felt like a dying person going to heaven. I was flying!

Finally I realized I was on my bike actually, well and truly flying! I was stunned but the whole gang was watching me, so I started acting cool again.

My bike on its own did a three-sixty and then a loop the loop. As I realized I couldn't fall I did more daring tricks. Cockroach, Tawny and Slug were gaping. Spider had actually fainted! Spike was yelling "Way'da go George! Do it again!" with much enthusiasm.

That set my mind thinking. I'd be in the newspaper, on TV, radio and the Guinness Book of Records! What fun to have a bike that could fly!

Georgia Miller (9) Bilgola Plateau PS

IN SPACE

One day I went to the moon. We went in a triangle shaped rocket. We saw lots of stars. My cat couldn't come. He had to go next door. We saw the moon. We had lots of fun. We floated everywhere.

Laura McWhinnie (6) Maroubra Junction PS

❧ MY FRIEND AND I IN SPACE ❧

Once upon a time there was a girl and her name was Genevieve. She was my best friend and she was 7 years old just like me. My birthday was in October and Genevieve's birthday was in September. We both wanted to go to space for our birthdays. So we went into the garden and started to play

astronauts. Suddenly, down from the sky came a rocket. So Genevieve and I jumped in the rocket and it started to go up and into the sky until it vanished into a cloud.

Genevieve was scared, so I put a parachute on her and I put her out the door. She went down, down, down. I had such fun, but I was lonely up in space.

Georgia Maddocks (7) Newport PS

❧ THE GREAT BUBBLEGUM BLOWOUT ❧

Paul looked, straining his eyes at the money his father was counting. It seemed like ages. Finally, Dad closed his wallet. "There you go, two dollars in change." He walked off to the lounge room.

Paul walked to his room and put the money in his money box, leaving forty cents. He placed the money box back on the shelf and ran out to the garage for his bike. He jumped on the bike and slowly pedalled out of the garage, down the driveway, out of the street. Paul lived in a quiet area of the suburb out from Bathurst.

He rode furiously through the streets to the local shopping centre. He chained his bike and walked to the store. Every week he took forty cents and bought himself some bubblegum. He looked at all the different flavours. There was one on the stand different from the rest. Paul read the pack, HUBBA BUBBA SUPER DOOPER SPECIAL BUBBLE GUM. Amazing effects. Only pack in the world. Banana flavoured, forty cents.

"Looks interesting," he said and grabbed it.

"Good morning Paul," said Mr. Jennings, the shop owner. "What kind are you getting this time?" He looked at the pack. "Oh that, came in with the box of banana bubblegum – weird."

Paul handed over his money. "See ya." He unlocked his

bike chain and tied it around the crossbar. Paul looked at the packet. "Might be poisonous, some maniac may have slipped it in the box," he thought. "Oh what the heck." He undid the wrapper, pulled out a piece of bubblegum and shoved it into his mouth. "Mnnnn," he mumbled, this was the best tasting banana flavoured bubblegum ever. He chewed and chewed and got ready to blow a bubble. He breathed in and then out and a nice neat bubble appeared from within the gum. But that wasn't all, after Paul had given up blowing it got bigger, it didn't stop. It kept on growing. The bubble became bigger and bigger. Paul tried to detach it from his mouth but he couldn't.

Soon the bubble was so big it lifted him off the ground. He rose so quickly that in minutes he was reaching the clouds. Paul was rising faster than an aircraft. Below him Paul could see crowds of people looking up. He looked around and saw the city, very distant but he saw it. Then he saw he was about to go through a thick cloud. For ages all he could see was white. It was becoming hard to breathe.

Finally he caught a glimpse of blue, then there he was again up above the clouds. He was soaked. His clothes were soggy, then to his surprise he realised he was still rising. He looked around for a while then . . . . . . blank.

When he awoke he couldn't see anything, everything was black with white spots. Below him was a round thing all white and blue, brown grey, red and green. Above him was a plain round thing all grey. Then to his surprise he realised he was above the earth, heading for the moon.

Meanwhile back on Earth, everything in Paul's town had changed. Police rescue squads, news reporters (finally), firemen and crowds of people were packed into the little country town. Paul had been up for two days, and already he was the main headline around the world. His picture was on all the magazine covers and movie producers had contracts ready for him when he came down.

But while all this was happening, over in the United States NASA was preparing a shuttle to go and rescue Paul up in space. In outer space Paul had found that the bubblegum provided him with oxygen. Whoever made this stuff was a genius. He began to try taking off the gum but it was no use. Suddenly he felt a grab on his shirt. He turned around. A body in white with a big pack on his back was pulling towards a space ship. It was the space shuttle.

But he was still going up. Nothing could stop him. The astronaut tried to pull him down but finally let go of him. The space crew tried lots of things to rescue him but it was hopeless. Finally the crew gave up and left for Earth.

Paul thought, then received a brainwave. Why not pop the bubble? He tried to pop it with his hands and when that didn't work, grabbed a long sharp metal rod which had been floating around him, and with the sharp end, tapped the bubble. BANG! No bubble, just bits of bubblegum over his face, and bits floating. He realised he was falling slowly back towards the earth. He blanked out.

When he awoke, he was back in the earth's atmosphere, but only just. He could see the clouds very small but getting bigger. Paul was gaining speed. The clouds soon became so big then he passed through them. It only took a few seconds. When he fell out, he was again soaked.

Paul was getting faster. Below him was a big city area. He recognised it as Sydney. He'd gone up and come down almost in a straight line.

Sydney below him became bigger. He closed his eyes and screamed. Meanwhile, in a little house in the city, little Danny was playing in his play-set with trampoline, swings and monkey bars. All of a sudden Danny saw an object falling towards him.

He ran into the house screaming, "Mummy there's a unifentidied frying objeck." But as you guessed, it was Paul. He bounced on the trampoline, breaking a few strings and rose back into the air. He came right into a shallow part of a local riverbank. He went right through the ground, then he stopped. He was in a deep hole which he had obviously made. Paul gripped the earth and started to climb, but he always fell. He was trapped in a hole half a kilometre deep with water from the river slowly dripping into it. What a way to die. Paul sighed.

Nicholas Cheesley (11) St John Bosco, Engadine

2001 – A SPACE TREK

The butterflies were still in our tummies as Phillip, James and myself were waiting for the final countdown for blast off. I had done this part of the trip many times before but after we had reached the space station for refuelling and a brief rest, the journey to another galaxy filled me with awe.

5, 4, 3, 2, 1, ignition. Lift off. The force was tremendous and there was that brief moment of blackout. When we came to, we set about our tasks. I made sure our first stage fuel tanks were jettisoned, then fired our rockets, altering course to pass by the moon and on to space station ASTRA.

Suddenly there was a tremendous thud and the space ship's emergency lights flashed on. I hurled my way back to the flight deck and screamed at James, "What happened?" Phillip appeared at the same time and we all strapped up again. He said it looked like an enormous asteroid which appeared from nowhere but whatever, it had propelled us at speed this craft had never done before.

I tried to gain control, fired our retro rockets in the hope of slowing us down but no use. All I can remember was the brilliant colours and patterns and speed, speed, speed. Then there was a calmness and a sky that was not familiar to me.

I knew we were being drawn down to a planet. A planet that looked purple. A planet we didn't know. We were still going down too fast so I tried the retro rockets again and this time they slowed us down.

There was vibration and a feeling of coming through a dust storm. Then it cleared and I could see the surface. To my amazement it looked like a runway ahead, no time to decide if good or bad. It had to be a landing first time. We were down.

The reading on the meter showed the air was similar to earth, so we opened the hatch and stepped down. The soil looked blue purple and blackened trees stood in the distance. Before we could speak, a vision appeared before us, shimmering white; I could sense I was being scanned but before I could say anything the form spoke to us in our own language.

"Welcome to NAGUOD, follow."

This we did and from the purple gloom, entered into a beautiful shining city of domes and tubes, with trees and waterfalls and friendly faces. No longer the vision but bodies like ourselves. We learned that they had visited our planet many times before.

They offered to repair our craft and we could leave in peace or stay. As James and Phillip had families they wanted to return home but I decided to stay and learn their knowledge and share mine. I waved goodbye and watched the craft disappear. I felt a pang and wondered if I had done the right thing, but as I looked around and saw this shining new world, I knew the learning in my life was just beginning.

Neil Dougan (9) Newport PS

MAGIC

❧ THE PEN THAT CHANGED COLOURS ❧

Ngày xưa có một cây viết của tiên trên trời rớt xuống tr ần gian, gần nhà quê.

Em bé trai Tùng, của nhà đó đi qua và thấy cây viết đó. Tùng nghĩ cái đó là cái cây và trồng cây đó gần nhà của Tùng.

Mỗi ngày Tùng tưới cây đó ba lần, và Tùng bỏ it' đất mới mỗi tháng. Từ từ cái cây đó mọc lên.

Một năm qua rồi cái cây đó mọc trái lạ lắm. Ở trong trái đó có một cái cây nhỏ đủ màu của nắng vàng. Tùng bức một trái đó và lấy cây ra. Chừng nào Tùng vẽ vô giấy, đủ máy ra giấy.

Tùng bán trái đó ở hội chợ. Một trái là ba đồng, Tùng bây giờ giàu lắm.

Once upon a time there was a fairy pen that fell down to the countryside.

A boy named Tung saw it, and thought that it was a tree, so he planted the pen near his home.

Every day Tung watered the "tree" three times, and put some new soil at the root once a month. The tree grew up day by day.

A year passed, then the tree gave unusual fruits. Inside each fruit there was a little plant that had colours of the sun-rays. Tung picked out a plant from a fruit, and used it as a pen. It gave many different colours on the paper.

Tung sold these fruits at the show, 3 dollars each. Now Tung is very rich.

MyPhuong Dang (12) Villawood North PS

❧ WINTER MUSIC ❧

Once upon a time in a beautiful glade lived an old man. He was so old, some people thought he was a wizard. Every winter he would write music and notes of beautiful music would float down the valley.

There was a young girl who wanted to know where he got his music from, but the old man would not tell. So one winter morning she went and found out. The old man would break off icicles and the wind would make the most beautiful sound and the old man would write it down.

Suddenly a cold hand took hold of her shoulder. "Oh!" she cried, but when she looked up she saw it was the old man. "Spying on me little girl, well since you're here come inside." When she got inside there were music papers everywhere!

Soon the old man died and the young girl took his place writing music, and every so often she would climb up the mountain and sing her favourite tune called The Hills So Sweet.

Kristin Westlake (7) Tanilba Bay PS

Once upon a time there was a boy who went into the lounge room and all his family was in there too. He got a hat for Christmas. It was a magic hat. They went outside. They made a Snowman and they put a scarf on him. They used a sharp stick and rocks for his eyes and mouth and then the boy put the hat on him and he came to life. They got sticks for his arms and made him Snowman legs and put them on him. He could run, jump and walk but there was only one thing wrong with him. He could not hear because he was deaf and didn't have any ears to hear with. The family did not know how to make Snowman ears but he did not worry, because he still was alive and had that beautiful brown hat.

Scott Bedford (7) Bellambi PS

❧ THE WIZARD'S BIRTHDAY PARTY ❧

At the Wizard's party
The strangest things occurred
The teapot grew a pair of wings
And sang just like a bird

The cups and saucers danced a jig
And so did all the spoons
Who on the silver fruit-dish
Tinkled merry tunes

The candles on the cake sent
Up fountains of bright stars
And from the Wizard's larder
Trooped all the big jam-jars

They formed a guard of honour
Around the Wizard's chair
A crock of apple jelly cried
"A happy birthday Sir"

The cake grew enormous
And from a tiny door
Fairies, elves and pixies
All began to pour

They skipped across the table
And around the room they flew
Singing "Happy birthday
Dear Wizard Wog to you!"

Katherine Wark (11) St John the Apostle, Florey

❧ THE UNKNOWN PLANET ❧

One night I was reading a book about the Unknown Planet. When I had finally finished I got out of bed to put the book away. After I had put my book away I looked at my watch. It was 12 o'clock. I ended up only getting five hours sleep.

The next day it was Saturday. On Saturday I stayed home. That night I thought I saw something gigantic moving in the bush (because we lived right next to the national park). That time I only got no hours sleep.

In the morning I started to investigate. Nearly as soon as I stepped into my cubby, I was launched off the ground by a big hairy hand.

The next thing I knew I was in the weirdest spot I'd ever been before.

Then suddenly I was falling again, this time for what seemed hours. I'm just going to skip on to when I landed or I could be here writing for pages and pages.

Well when finally I hit the ground with a bump! and a THUMP! and a big CALUMP! well I thought to myself I wonder where I am. But when I tried to find out, I couldn't move. I was totally stuck to the GROUND! I didn't know how it had happened so that should mean I don't know how to get out (and that's just what it did mean). As soon as I had time to think about that I was out of the slimy gooey stuff with a big enormous PUFF of smoke!

There before my eyes I saw a magnificent gigantic wizard. He said that he would turn me into a frog. I didn't believe that. Then he said that he would turn me into a potato. Now I didn't believe *that*. But just then with a big mack and a whack on the back he turned me into a potato.

Then I said to him, "What am I?" He said that I was a NIT WIT! But then to get myself out of this state (which might be quite hard). Just then I was smuggled high off the ground by a giant furry hand.

The next thing I knew I was lying down in the hammock outside my house.

Stephen Gero (7) Kincumber PS

❧ ALFRED'S MAGIC ❧

Alfred had met Raldeen the sorcerer at the battle of Castle Orgnay. After seeing Raldeen's display of powers he became very curious and interested in his magic. So Alfred approached Raldeen and asked if he would take him on as an apprentice. Raldeen was not at all surprised at this and took him on immediately.

From then on Alfred underwent a rigorous training of mind and body. When Raldeen thought he was ready he taught Alfred the set-down spells and made him revise them until he knew them off by heart. When he knew all this Raldeen told him of the most powerful and dangerous part of magic, Mind Sense.

As Alfred was walking in the Keep of the castle Orgnay, where he was being trained, he saw his master and teacher coming towards him.

"I have just been thinking about you and your magical talents. I have come to the conclusion that you have the ability to become a full sorcerer, though I know not how great you shall be. Your training as a sorcerer shall now begin in earnest." The sorcerer paused for a while.

Alfred had thought that his training was almost over and even Raldeen had said that there was only one more thing that he had to learn. He felt Raldeen's mind feeling his thoughts and he tried to block them out but he couldn't.

"Don't worry so lad, there is only one more thing to learn. The thing that separates an apprentice from a full sorcerer is Mind Sense. The ability that lets your mind leave your body to search ahead."

Then Raldeen led Alfred into his private magical library where he gave Alfred a sorcery lesson that lasted well into the early hours of the morning. Alfred read many chapters of many books, but mostly just sat and listened to what Raldeen had to say. To finish off the evening, Alfred had a go at it, but he only explored a few rooms of the Keep and it was all under Raldeen's control. As he was leaving he thought that he might try it out by himself the next day, but Raldeen read his thoughts.

"You know all that I can tell you, but you do not have practical knowledge of using this power and if you try to use it now you shall almost certainly lose your way," Raldeen warned him harshly.

As soon as he got to his chamber, Alfred dropped onto his bed and fell into a deep sleep.

The next morning Alfred rose at the crack of dawn and against Raldeen's advice he fell into a trance and let his mind wander. Down the Keep stairs, into the courtyard, out through the drawbridge and into the countryside. After a few minutes the light was gone and a mist appeared. At first he thought it was real mist, but he could feel the sunlight and clear skies above him. He panicked!

Back at the castle a guard had found Alfred but couldn't wake him. They called Raldeen and as soon as he saw him he knew what was wrong. He sat down, left his body behind and followed Alfred's thoughts. When Alfred felt Raldeen's presence the fog lifted and he could find his way back.

When back, Raldeen turned to him.

"After that display I think you have learned a lesson and are now a full and proper sorcerer. BUT! I have some advice for you. When you are mind-travelling look for a green sort of light that will always keep you on the right path."

Kurt Fienberg (10) Scone PS

GHOSTS

❧ THE GHOST BABY AND THE GHOST MOTHER ❧

Once I saw a house. I looked in and I saw a baby ghost. The baby ghost said, "Gooo gaaa gooo gaaa gooo gaaaa Mummy." The door opened and I went in. The baby ghost ran to her mother. The mother said, "Who opened the door?" "A person," I said. "Go back home," she said. "Can we make friends?" I said. "No," said the mother ghost.

Justin Mercer (6) St Edward's, Tamworth

❧ FRANKY AND ME ❧

One day I was walking in the paddock with my friend Karen, when suddenly I froze. Karen stopped and turned around.

"What's the matter?" she asked.

"Look!" I pointed.

Karen had one look and ran.

"Come back," I shouted but it was no good, she kept running. I kept walking towards the flashing light flying in the air. As I got closer I could see that the strange light was a lamp and as the lamp moved I could see footprints on the ground. I was about to turn and run but I decided to find out what was going on. As fast as I could I ran up and took the lamp. As I ran I heard footsteps following me but suddenly the sun started to come up and the footprints were no longer there. I knew I should have asked Brianna to come with me tonight, at least she would have stayed with me I thought. I kept running until I was home.

"Where have you been?" asked Mum.

"For a walk," I answered.

"What time did you leave?"

"Four a.m." I said.

"Go to your room until I tell you to come out and next time ask."

I hid the lamp under my bed. I was in my room for half an hour.

"Mum, can I come out now?" I shouted.

"I suppose. Have you done your homework?" Mum asked.

"No, I don't have homework on weekends," I answered. "Can I please go to Brianna's house?" I asked.

"No, not today, Sally."

I went to my room and put on my tape recorder as loud as it would go, then I climbed out the window and went to Brianna's house. I told Brianna what had happened but she didn't believe me.

"Do you want to sleep at my house?" I asked.

"OK," said Brianna. "I'll just ask Mum."

Brianna's mum said she could but she had to be home before lunch the next day. When we got home I told Brianna to count to twenty, then knock at the door because by the time she had finished counting I could be inside.

"1, 2, 3, 4, 5, 6, 7, 8, 9, 10, 11, 12, 13, 14, 15, 16, 17, 18, 19, 20," she counted. KNOCK, KNOCK.

"I'll get it," I yelled. "Mum, it's Brianna. Can she stay and play?" I asked.

"Yes," Mum answered.

"Mum, could Brianna sleep tonight?"

"I'll think about it," said Mum. "OK."

"Could I go and help her get her stuff?"

"Yes, but be home by five."

We got Brianna's stuff and went home. By the time we had finished the game we were playing it was time to have tea. When we had finished Mum said we could have the house to ourselves because she and Dad were going to Bingo and after that they were staying at Mum's friend's to help her look after her new baby.

"Bye," they shouted as they went out the door. We sat down and watched TV. After that we went to bed because we were tired.

"Goodnight," I said.

"Yeah, goodnight," Brianna said.

After a while Brianna asked me if I could sleep.

"No," I whispered.

Suddenly I heard the door open.

"Is that you, Mum?"

There was no answer.

"Dad, stop trying to scare me."

But still no answer.

"Who could it be?" Brianna asked.

"I don't know," I said shivering. Suddenly I heard footsteps coming down the hall.

"Are you scared?" Brianna asked.

"No, are you?" I whispered.

"No," she answered but I know she was and so was I.

"Why did you take my lamp?" a voice said.

"Brianna, is that you?" I whispered but all I heard was snoring. Oh no! She must have fallen asleep. She's as bad as Karen, I thought.

"What's your name?" the voice said.

"Sally," I answered shivering. "Who are you?" I asked.

"I'm Franky, the ghost," the voice replied. "Why did you steal my lamp?"

"I'm sorry," I said, frightened.

"Could I please have it back then?" Franky said.

I didn't say anything because I was still shivering.

"Don't be frightened," Franky said. "I won't hurt you. I want to be your friend."

"Where are you? I can't see you, it's too dark. Can I turn on the light?" I asked.

"Yes, of course, but you still won't be able to see. I'm a ghost, remember?"

"I'll still turn it on so I can get your lamp for you. There you go."

"I'll have to go now," said Franky.

"Please stay so I can introduce you to Brianna," I said.

"No, don't wake her up. You can introduce us tomorrow. Bye."

And that was the last I ever saw of him.

Sally Newman (11) Deniliquin South PS

❧ STRANGE ADVENTURE ☙

It was a moonlit night in winter. Snow fell softly on the car's roof and windscreen, pitta patta pitta patta. The car approached a sharp turn in Ranger's Canyon.

Not another car in sight. The next city was six miles away. I turned around the bend, and there the headlights picked up a silhouette by the side of the road. When I got a bit closer I noticed it was a girl in her late teens. She ran out in front of the car waving her arms wildly. I stopped the car and offered her a lift.

"Thank you," she said with grateful eyes. My mind wondered on how she got there and why was she out on a night like this.

I asked her where she lived. She replied, "4104 Kelly's Street."

It must have been about ten minutes before I realised that the girl had disappeared – only the mark of her joggers on the floor was left.

Shocked and amazed I drove on. When I reached the city I drove to 4104 Kelly's Street. I stopped the car and walked up to the door. I knocked on the door and an old lady answered it. I poured out the whole story to her. When I had finished she said, "Yes, that was my daughter. She got lost in the Canyon eighteen years ago today. Every year on this date a traveller calls to say that a girl said she lived at this street but she disappeared in my car." With that she shut the door.

Slowly I walked back to my car. Another car whizzed by.

Monique Power (11) Dubbo South PS

This is an old spooky house with some bats in it and it is dark.

Timothy Vanderwerf (6) St Philomena's, Moree

71

WITCHES

A witch came to my birthday party and ate all my cake.

Casey Shorter (5) Scotts Head PS

❧ WICKED WITCHES' SPELL ❧

One platypus's nose and a dragon's tongue.
Spider's leg and a bird's wing.
Stir them together and drink it slowly.
You will turn into a red back spider.

Amy Cannon (5) Bankstown West PS

❧ WITCH, WITCH ❧

"Witch, witch, when do you fight?"
"Over the hill on a Saturday night."
"Witch, witch, what do you make?"
"Ice cream cake with jelly and snake."
"Witch, witch, where do you fly?"
"Over the sky where skeletons die."
"Witch, witch, where are you fat?"
"Over my body and under my hat."

Alexandra Hill (7) Balgowlah Heights PS
(innovation on "Witch, Witch" by R. Fyleman)

❧ A WICKED WITCH ❧

Once upon a time there was a witch.
She had a cat.
Every day some milk was delivered and she always got some.
There was a cat and a rabbit next door and they got milk too.
But the witch always got up really early and took the milk off the other animals.
One day the witch slept in.
When the milkman came he knew that the wicked witch lived in that house, so he tipped the milk on her.
It poured, and poured and poured on that witch and she sure woke up.
Then the cat ran and licked the milk happily.

Katherine Leach (7) Bexley North PS

Melissa Kelly (6) Balgowlah Heights PS

THE NIGHT I SHRANK!

Last night when I couldn't sleep I looked at the window. I saw a broomstick, a witch was flying on it. I couldn't believe my eyes. I ran outside to see. The broomstick stopped and landed at my gate. The witch walked up to me and said "Little little girl I have some sweets for you."

I was hungry so I took the sweets, then something happened. I started to feel funny. I was shrinking, I looked up and the witch was gone. I grew smaller and smaller and smaller until I was the size of a cockroach. I went back to my room, I couldn't reach it so I sat on my shoe and went to sleep. In the morning I woke up, I was very hungry. I heard my mum calling "Anna where have you been?"

I ran to her and called as loud as I could, my mum saw me. She said "Oh my dear is this Anna?" I called out "Yes Mama."

She bent down and picked me up and put me on the table. I told her about the witch and the sweets. It was good that she believed me. My mum took me to my father and told him all about it. My little brother came in and said "Where is Anna?" Dad told him what happened. Quickly my mother suggested that we should go to the doctors. When we got there the doctor said that he didn't know how to make me well. So we went home. I just ate two little grains of rice. I had to sleep in my shoe. I couldn't sleep so I ran out and sat on the ground. A witch came, but this one was different. She said that she was the other witch's sister. She gave me the medicine. As I drank it I grew bigger and bigger. I ran to my dad and told him. In the morning we were all happy.

Anna Chau (9) Lidcombe PS

WITCH'S MIXTURE

Fat frog, thin frog
Mutilated mashed.
Minced frog, roasted frog
Salty frog hashed.

Warm bat, cool bat
Bat over ice.
Stewed bat, sizzled bat
Bat served with spice.

Bitter snail, battered snail
Sliced snail stew.
Leg of snail, loin of snail
Insect Cordon Bleu.

Danielle Sauer (11) Woodburn Central

The old witch slowly walked over to the big pot of bubbling, hot, colourful stew and stirred it slowly, looking at it blankly. Then it made popping, squirting noises and spat. The witch stood back and looked horrified as it overflowed and came crawling towards her.

The stew was a browny-green colour which made growling, snorting noises as it squirmed towards the witch. As if the stew had eyes it came towards her. As it did it began to grow taller and form into a ghost-type shape made from stew. The witch's stringy hair stood on end, her eyes were like saucepans and her body stood still in the corner of the room, shocked with fright.

The stew or monster, should I say, put its squirmy body around the witch's and pulled her towards a cage made from rotten bones!! "No. No. You can't do this," yelled the witch, finding herself being pushed into the cage.

The stew just growled louder and locked the cage with a skeleton key and threw it out the old, cracked window.

The witch eyed the stew, watching it carefully, but not really worrying much now, knowing that she could put the stew under a spell. The stew was busily taking things off the dusty shelves and pouring a bit of this and that in the pot.

The witch waved her hands about, and out loud she said "Kincho, Mincho, Lincho, Demincho."

"Growl, Growl," yelled the stew as it began to float up to the ceiling. Then all of a sudden it came falling down like a popped balloon.

Meanwhile the witch magicked herself out of the cage and put the stew back in the pot. Then she threw the pot and stew out the window but didn't notice the one blob still left on the floor.

In the morning the witch woke with a sudden shock of finding the stew growling over her bed! The witch screamed in anger and fright and ran out of her bed in her nighty down the stairs. Tumbling to her feet she burst out the door and jumped on her broomstick. It wouldn't go! She looked behind her. The stew was coming. She jumped on the broom and it flew off not knowing where it was going because the driver was looking at the stew and panicking and didn't see the tree!

"OW!" screamed the witch and with the sudden bump she fell off the broomstick and landed in the nearby pond.

The stew giggled loudly and peered over the edge of the pond. The witch's clothes were rising to the surface of the water but the witch was nowhere to be seen. The only thing left of the witch was the echoing screams as the witch hit the water.

"All is well that ends well," chuckled the stew as it headed back to take over the witch's old house!!

Caroline Ofner (10) Wenona, North Sydney

FAIRIES

❧ THE TEDDY BEAR AND THE FAIRY ❧

Once upon a time there was a teddybear factory. It was a night when the factory was closed. There was a little fairy passing by the factory. The little fairy saw a little light so she went to see what the light was. At first she was afraid but she flew over to the back door. She opened the door and saw a teddybear. She picked him up and brought him to life and asked him, "Why aren't you in a box?" "Because a woman stitched me up the wrong way and put my eyes the wrong way." "Well how would you like to stay with me?" "I'd love to! But what if I can't? What if the government doesn't let me?" "Ha, ha, ha, I don't live on Earth. I live in heaven with God and the Angels." "Then I'll come." "Okay, let's go." So they flew back to heaven and the little teddybear said, "I love it here."

Socrates Menegakis (8) Campsie PS

❧ THE SNOW FAIRY ❧

One day we went for a walk in the snow. There was so much to see. I didn't see that my mum and dad were a long way ahead of me. I started to cry. A snow fairy came along. She said, "What is the matter?" I said, "I have lost my mum and dad." "I can help you," said the snow fairy. She got her wand out. She made a spell. "Snow, snow, bring me a magic carpet!"

There was a mat sitting on the snow. "Sit on the mat," said the snow fairy. "Soon we will be home." Suddenly we were off. We stopped for a drink at a pond.

Suddenly a strange noise was coming close. A snowman came to us.

"Get out of here!" yelled the snowman. He started to throw snowballs. We jumped on the mat and started to fly. I could see our house. "Look," I said, "there is my house!"

"I will take you there," she said.

We flew in the window of the lounge room. The snow fairy said goodbye.

I heard a knock at the door. It was mum and dad.

"Hi!" I said.

They looked surprised because I was already home.

Clare Dunne (6) Figtree PS

❧ THE FLOWER FAIRY AND THE LEAF FAIRY ❧

One day Sweet Pea looked up and saw a face looking at her. I must come here every day she thought. That night Sweet Pea went home still puzzled over the face.

Early next morning Sweet Pea found a note on the door. It was from Osman. The note read, "Dear fairy, I was the one you saw yesterday. My name is Osman. Please meet me at the birdbath at twelve o'clock today. From Osman."

Sweet Pea could hardly wait. Come eleven thirty, Sweet Pea had her shower and brushed her hair. At last the clock struck twelve and Sweet Pea set off.

When she arrived she could see nothing at first, but then, out of the bushes, stepped a beautiful leaf fairy. The leaf fairy, of course, was Osman.

"Are you Osman?" stammered Sweet Pea.

"Yes. I'm Osman," replied Osman.

Sweet Pea invited Osman to tea that night. For dinner they had honey-cake (one of Sweet Pea's best recipes). Just then there was a tap at the door. It was the Robin Redbreast.

"The butterfly is holding a grand feast and wants you to come," the Robin Redbreast told them. "The feast is to be held at the birdbath at one o'clock on Saturday." The Robin Redbreast flew off without another word.

A storm started blowing up. "You'd better sleep here tonight," Sweet Pea warned Osman. That night Osman lay with Sweet Pea in her little bed, listening to the wind and the rain pelting down on the roof. Soon they fell asleep.

When morning came, Osman woke first. "Wake up, Sweet Pea. Wake up," she said. "We have to collect the things for the dresses that we are going to wear."

The sun was fully in the sky by the time they set out. First they went to Sweet Pea's flower bed and picked some of her flowers. Then they went to Osman's tree and found some good leaves.

Osman and Sweet Pea went to their little houses to sew their dresses. Osman and Sweet Pea were kept busy right up to the Saturday morning.

That day, at twelve o'clock, Sweet Pea put on her frock, all tied with ribbons and set off to the feast. On the way she met Osman and they walked to the feast hand in hand.

Natalie Crowther (8) Fisher PS

❧ THE BURNING CANDLE ❧

There was a terrifying storm. Lightning split through the black sky and thunder crashed against the house which shook. I lost my balance and fell over. Everything went black. You could hear shrieks from my little sister upstairs.

I knew what it was. It was a blackout so I didn't worry about it.

I got a candle from up high and lit it. I lit some more for my two brothers and sister. I hopped into bed and went on with the novel I was reading.

The candle was burning low and everything was fairly quiet except for the rain and thunder.

The candle now was about to go out and I heard a whisper. I got out of bed and the whisper I heard was getting stronger. "It's just the rain" I told myself, but it wasn't. I went over to the candle. There I saw a tiny, tiny, tiny little figure wandering about my bedside table. I went up to the figure and then I knew what the whisper was. I found it to be a piece of wax with legs and arms.

"Hello," I said. "What is . . . is your name and wh-where do you come from?" I added uneasily.

"Well my name is Ellyphelfie and I come from this candle right next to me. As you see I'm a piece of wax which comes from the candle. And tell me who are you?" Ellyphelfie said in his tiny voice.

"I am called Sophie and I live in this house," I said stumbling to find words.

I took the creature from my bedside table gently onto my finger and then examined it. "Hey what are you doing to me?" said Ellyphelfie.

"Oh sorry, am I hurting you? I was just wondering what that glowing stuff on you is."

Then I realised that the candle was out and the glowing stuff was lighting the room up. I put Ellyphelfie back in a box and put the remains of the burnt candle with him, and went on reading my book thinking about Ellyphelfie.

Catherine Boyd (9) Wenona, North Sydney

TWO POEMS

❧ R E D ❧

Red is a flame
flickering, flaming.
Red is a bushfire
swaggering, swaying.
Red curls around you
in a dark, heated room.
Red is a tomato,
an apple with a worm.
Red are the shadows
of fiery torches.
Red is a billowing mountain of fire
which tumbles and scorches.
Red is a cardinal,
a bright, witty fox.
Red is not knowing
what's in that box.
Red is a ruby
with a rosy glow.
Red is the feeling
of standing up in front of everybody
and not knowing what to say
on the big day.
Red is the end
of a fabulous film.
Red is a raspberry drink

filled up to the brim.
Red is the sun
huge and powerful.
Red is goodbye
to your best friend.

Luke Mynott (10) Normanhurst West PS

❧ MISTY ❧

I am Misty,
Girl of the mists,
Sister to shadows,
Daughter of darkness,
She who treads on untrodden ways,
Teller of tales and wayfarer upon
The wilder shores of midnight.

Welcome to my midnight world,
Thrice welcome, be you venturesome stranger
Or one who has fled the dark at the top of the stair
Or long familiar, treasured, trusted friend —
All have trod the misty ways
And come to me for courage.
The hidden things, the darkling fantasticals,
And all the unbidden creatures of the night
Forsake the secret places,
The last and uttermost outposts
Beyond imagination, beyond compare
And come to me as I wander
Lone upon the strand, lone upon the shore,

Beside the sea of loneliness,
Moon-silvered, mist-kissed,
Listening,
Glistening.
Welcome, mortals all, welcome mystics,
Thrice welcome.
Is that your heart I hear beating in the silence?
Or something else? Or something other?
Fear not, touch my hand.
Tread boldly in my world,
My world of darkness,
For fear cannot endure
In Misty's presence.

Since last we met
I have wandered the world
From my Cavern of Dreams.
I have crossed the Mountains of Mystery,
To the Wilderness of Willows,
Drunk at the Pool of Life,
Traversed the midnight darkness of the world,
Pieced History, shrunk distance,
Gathering garlands of grimness
And tales of the other world
Till now told only to the air,
And fashioned them all
For your shiversome delight
Into tales beyond explanation,
Things without a name
To pause and ponder on
In hours before the dawn.

The bats fly high
Against the moon,
Pipistrella flitting,
Radar gliding,
Wrapt in silence, watching
As we gather here
Until the mists shall come again,
Knowing Mist shatters fear.
For things that wait in the darkness
The things that wait for you,
The name of every single one is fear,
And fear is banished from my domains.
So look upon the wonders I show you,
Look at them and pause,
Enjoy your shivers,
But touch my hand and no harm shall touch you,
Touch my hand and tread boldly
Along these untrodden ways,
Wrap my misty mantle about you,
And fear cannot come near.

And remember,
I am Misty,
Girl of mists,
Sister of shadows,
Daughter of darkness,
She who treads on untrodden ways,
Teller of tales and wayfarer upon
The wilder shores of midnight.

Belinda Fielding (11) Newport PS

SHORT STORIES

❧ THE LITTLE SCREW ❧

Once upon a time there was a little car. It was owned by Faye Kuch. One day Faye had to go to Newcastle to have it fixed and she left a screw on the back bumper bar. She started the car and went and the little screw held on tight. Faye went over some bumps and the little screw held on even tighter.

Its hair was blowing in the wind and it said, "Oh dear, if Faye doesn't stop and get me off, I'm going to fall off and get squashed." With that it slipped and fell. It tried to climb up a little higher. It got up and held on even tighter. Then Faye turned a sharp corner and the screw held on even tighter.

"Oh help!" said the screw as Faye went up a steep hill and down and turned another corner. "Oh dear, oh dear!" It tried to hold on to a piece of string but it wasn't secure so it fell right back to where it had started.

So it started again. 1,2,3,4,5,6,7 steps it climbed. 8,9,10! It made it up on the bumper bar again. It jumped up and down happily. Silly screw! It jumped so high that it nearly fell right off. But luckily it grabbed on to the bumper bar again.

"Phew! I nearly had a fall!" Faye turned one more corner and stopped at a big white house with a shed beside it. Then Faye remembered the screw and when she looked at the bumper bar it was still there. She and her mother laughed and the little screw laughed too.

Anna Kuch (7) Avondale SDA Primary, Cooranbong

❧ A DAY IN THE LIFE OF MRS SPONGE ❧

The kitchen cupboard door silently opened and a beam of sunlight fell perfectly upon me, a torn, old kitchen sponge. Susie, a ten year old girl, then put her hand in the cupboard to grab a sponge to wash up the breakfast dishes. Beside me was a brand new sponge wrapped in sparkling cellophane.

Of course, she was forced to choose me because her mother would be angry if she didn't. You could tell Susie really wanted to use the new one by the scowling expression on her face. She reached in and ripped me off the shelf, squeezing me so tight I nearly choked.

She threw me in the scorching hot water. As I hit the water sudsy bubbles flew everywhere. Susie dumped in the breakfast plates. They were *GREASY* with bacon fat and egg yolk. Here was I an aged sponge being asked to face all this. I had a feeling this was going to be terrible.

As I was wiped across the plate the egg yolk and fat was caked into me. It got caught in my crevices until the scorching hot water dissolved the fat.

The whole experience was disgusting.

Finally she finished but not so the disgusting experiences! She forgot to let the water out. It gradually got colder and colder until I thought I would get pneumonia.

It was about an hour before Susie's mum got home and let the water out — Boy was I glad to see her! GURGLE!, GULP!, DRIBBLE!, DRIP!, DRIP! What glorious sounds!

She squeezed me out and put me on the warm window sill. The sunshine was so welcome after the cold greasy water.

I could see the dog chasing the cat up the tree.

Before I knew it I was asleep, dreaming of the days when I was brand new and "UNOPENED"!

Rachel Corben (10) Goonellabah PS

❧ THE PROWLER ❧

Suddenly I woke up. I looked at my watch using the light on the side to see. It was 12:10.

"That must be wrong," I thought. "It seemed only a minute ago that I hopped into bed and went to sleep."

Feeling confused I jumped out of bed and went downstairs to see what the time was on the micro-wave because I knew it was always correct. When I reached the bottom of the steps I was very surprised to see the micro-wave showed that the time was 12:10. It was then I started wondering what had woken me, because I never wake up at night. I crept all the way back to my room, crashing into the brick wall and tripping over twice.

Just as I jumped into bed and turned off my light I heard a noise. It was frightening, and very different from the singing of birds or the rustling of the wind in the branches of the great oak trees. (Or any other trees for that matter!) This noise sounded more like someone sawing through wood. I listened carefully and heard it once again. All of a sudden I thought that someone was on the roof with a huge saw trying to cut a hole in the roof so that they could come in.

I listened until I heard the noise again and put my chair directly underneath it. After that I put my roller-skates next to my chair and opened my door. I set those three traps so that when he or she entered they would step onto the chair, thinking it was the floor. When they took their next step they would fall on the roller-skates, roll out the door and smash into the brick wall.

When I had finished the traps, I crept quietly up to Mum and Dad's room and told them everything. Dad called the family together while Mum and I went downstairs to find a torch. We all went outside, rugged up in our gowns and slippers, to see what the noise was. I shone the torch at the roof to see . . . two cats fighting.

"Some prowler!" said my brother and sister at the same time.

Lisa Croudace (10) Pennant Hills PS

❧ AN EMBARRASSING SITUATION ❧

It was terrible. Of all people it just had to happen to me. A kid in my class, Bill (some people call him Billy the Kid), said I didn't have the courage to venture out into the bush by myself at night. I challenged him but knew that William (he hates being called William so I'll call him that for the rest of the story) would be brave enough to do anything. I was determined to cross the bush from one side to the other. The date set was the fourteenth of April, my birthday.

I set out at ten at night. Through the corner of my eyes, I saw someone following me. With teeth chattering and body shivering, I entered the dark and eerie scrub. Voices could be heard ahead of me. Two people in black were visible in the distance. They both carried two bags in each hand. All at once a single thought struck me. They were both robbers.

For some strange reason I could see lights. Thinking there might be more than those two thieves, I crept up to them and jumped on one.

Suddenly a voice said, "Cut, cut. This isn't in the script. Hey kid, what did you do that for? Get off the set before I throw you off."

I turned around. All around me were rifles (which are long microphones) cameras and workers on a movie set. I had interrupted the screening of a film. How embarrassing! Feeling very redfaced I muttered, "Gee, I'm terribly sorry."

Steven Gibbs (11) Eastwood PS

"Fantasy" *Christine Manalo (10) Leichhardt PS*

Juliett Ramsey (11) Currambena, Lane Cove

"The Friendship" *Riley Cox (7) Warrawee PS*

"Sailing Boats" *Rosemary Ravese (8) Mt Pritchard PS*

"Looking after God's Garden"   *Year 1 (5-6) Covenant Christian School, Belrose*

❧ TAKEN BY SURPRISE ❧

Excitement filled my heart as I grew nearer to my letter box. I had been expecting a letter from the Royal Australian Ballet Company for weeks. Samantha and I had written to them asking if we could audition for their new ballet — "The Tales of White Tails." Samantha is my friend. She and I grew up with each other. Now we both have the same interests, the main one being ballet.

I opened the letter. Sure enough, in three weeks time we were to audition for the ballet. The first thing I did after I had read this was to ring Sam. She sounded pretty excited too. We talked it over and made all the arrangements for transport. Realising that we hadn't got much time to train, we got off the phone.

Weeks passed, each day with more and more training. All too soon came the day of the audition. After Sam's parents had dropped us off outside the auditorium, we both walked slowly and very nervously up the stairs to the great room. Laughter filled the room as we stepped in. Were they laughing at us? No, actually I think they were just excited like us. Sam and I joined in too. Silence fell over us all as Mr Steega, the organiser of the audition, stepped in. After a long talk and a lot of organisation, we were finally ready. In groups of four we went to the centre of the floor and did our warm-ups and centre work. Our warm-ups consist of mainly exercises. That is not all. After everyone had gone through this, we were taken one by one into a tiny room at the back of the auditorium. There, we were examined. Mr Steega had a gruff voice and I tried to avoid speaking to him. I did my barre work in complete silence. As I made my way to the door he spoke to me. He frightened me so much I jumped ten feet! To think he scared me so much and he only wanted to tell me to get the next person. Sam was waiting outside and I sent her in. She came out of the tiny room wearing a grin. She came over to me. We both grabbed our gear and raced outside. Waiting for us outside were my parents. "How was it, girls?" — neither of us replied.

About five weeks after the audition I received a letter. I tried to guess who it was from. At first I thought it was from my penfriend in Auckland. Then I realised. It was from the Australian Ballet Company. I carefully opened it. I read it over five times because the first time I couldn't believe what it said. I soon got it into my head that it was true. I had made it into the ballet! I picked up the phone and rang Sam. She sounded very disappointed. "I got in" I said. She didn't answer. Sam hung up so I decided to hang up as well.

My first practice was in three days time. Fortunately Sam had got over her disappointment and was going to come and watch my first lesson. That lesson was great and so were all the others!

Jennifer Behr (10) Lane Cove West PS

❧ MOSES THE STORYTELLER ❧

My favourite story that Moses the storyteller told me was the story about the singing drum.

The story began like this. A long time ago there was a little girl who had a beautiful voice. One day when she was fetching water she began to sing. The Zimbi heard her singing, so he crept up behind her and put her in his drum. Then the Zimbi said to her, "When I beat my drum you must sing or I will belt you."

"Yes," the little girl replied, as she was shivering with fright.

Zimbi walked to the nearest village and played the drum so the girl began to sing. When the villagers heard the beautiful singing they came out of their huts to listen. After the little girl had finished singing, the Zimbi said, "I am hungry, I am thirsty."

When the villagers heard this they went and fetched mangoes, oranges, bananas, beans, fresh goats milk and honey beer. After he finished he let out a big belch, "Erp!" When nobody was looking, he threw four beans into the drum for the girl to eat, then he had a sleep.

Next day the girl's mother and father heard about the little girl. So that night they took the girl out of the drum and filled it with bees. When the Zimbi found out she would not sing, he took the drum into the bush and took the top off. The bees stung him so badly that he ran into the bush and was never seen again.

Laura Fabrello (9) Winston Hills PS

❧ MISS LIN THE SEA GODDESS ❧

In a small province in China, there lived a family by the name of Lin. They lived by the shores of the Eastern Sea and were poor fisher-folk. They had a daughter whom they loved more than precious jade, and two sons who helped their father with the fishing.

Like all women in those days, Miss Lin occupied the time during which her father and brothers were away, with spinning, weaving and embroidery.

As Miss Lin sat with her mother at the midday meal one day, she began to feel unusually drowsy and sleepy. But although she tried hard to keep awake, she eventually fell into a deep sleep; and while she slept, her head was filled with a strange dream. She dreamt that the dragon brothers who lived under the sea were angry. There were five dragon brothers, all of them more than a mile in length, and when they all lashed their tails together, mountains would crumble and fall, while the waves rose to such a height that they nearly touched the sky; and hurricanes occurred when the five sea dragons flew up into the heavens.

Miss Lin, in her dream, saw the rains beating down upon the ocean and the waves rise high, towering over the small fishing crafts which held her beloved father and brothers. And her dream was so real and life-like, that she thought she could hear the wild winds shrieking across the ocean.

Then she saw herself running from their small house and into the water, seizing the rope which was tied to her father's boat. She put that rope between her teeth and seized the other ropes which were fastened to the boats of her brothers with her hands. Quickly, she dragged and pulled at the three ropes towards the land.

While she was doing that in her dreams, the young Lin maiden groaned and cried out in real life. Her mother, alarmed by her daughter's moans, shook her and asked her what was wrong from time to time, to awaken her to find out what the matter was. Miss Lin heard her mother's voice in her dreams, but as she opened her mouth to reply to her mother's questions, the rope which was fastened to her father's boat slipped from her mouth and her father's boat disappeared from the surface, never to be seen again.

On her awakening, the young maiden related to her mother what she had dreamt. Late that night, the two brothers returned with sad tidings. Their father's boat had been lost and they feared that he had gone down to the realms of the Sea Dragons.

Poor Miss Lin put the blame upon herself for not saving her father as she did her two brothers in her dream. She ran out onto the shore, where her mother saw her plunge into the dark waters in search of her lost father.

But search as they would, they could not find her. None of her family or anyone else ever saw her again on the face of the earth, but her brothers and other sailors often saw her image out at sea whenever there was a storm and each time they reached land safely.

Perhaps the five sea brothers had taken the young maiden in to watch over sailors at sea.

Retold by Siew Jin Ooi (11) John Purchase PS, Cherrybrook

❧ THE LUCKY ESCAPE ❧

One stormy night, I was in the bedroom with my mother, she told me a story about the day we left Vietnam. This is the story.

In 1979 at night time our relatives and our family went to the open sea in a small boat. We took everything we needed.

After a couple of days in the sea there was a terrible storm. The sea became very rough. Almost every person began to vomit and feel sick. My little brother, Huy, was always happy and so was I.

After three days and nights, our boat approached the Malaysian sea. From the far horizon, we saw a navy ship coming towards us and all the people aboard were scared, but the captain of the navy ship was friendly. From his ship he tied a rope to our boat in case the small, crowded boat sank. Then he pulled our boat for a while, but we decided to follow them instead of being pulled. At lunch time they gave us food to eat and that was delicious.

By evening we reached Indonesia and stayed at a place called Carremute. Some people slept on the boat and as for others, they slept on the porch of a house. Only my family was lucky to sleep in the house of a Chinese family, but there wasn't room for my father and grandmother, so they had to stay outside.

We stayed there for three days and on the third day our boat had to move to another place, Letung, on the same island.

It was raining hard. We slept in front of the shops and that night it rained very heavily again. We all got soaked.

In the morning my mother wanted to find somewhere for our family to stay. At last she found a house but she couldn't speak Indonesian so she tried to tell the lady by moving her hands.

We stayed there for ten days, then went to another place. There were no people living there. When we arrived we built some hay houses for shelter. Before long there were over ten thousand refugee people living there. We didn't have enough medicine and some people were very sick. Some even died. Each day we had to line up to get one can of rice and some other food but it wasn't enough so we had to go fishing.

As the days went by we got more food. The first five months we had a hard time but after that it was better.

My family and some other families went to Penang. After a couple of days an Australian had an interview with us and let us settle in Australia. Then we went on a big ship to Singapore. A few days later my mother had a baby boy and our family was very happy. We went to the zoo there and did lots of nice things.

After one month of waiting we finally arrived in Australia on 22nd February, 1980. That was the "Lucky Escape." Now we are very happy to live in Australia with freedom.

Thu Nguyen (10) Concord West PS

❧ SARAH GREENFIELD ❧

It was Tuesday. Sarah plodded home. This had been easily the worst day of her life. To start she had arrived from England only six hours ago. Things had been comfortable in her snug home in Yorkshire. Now everything had changed. First, she was to start a new school. Her teacher would be an ominous, strict man, Mr Wheeler.

The next day she packed her bag, kissed her mother goodbye, and trudged off to school. When she rounded a corner she saw a building. It was made of grey stone and the two towers on either side seemed to be saying, "Go away, we don't want you, English kid." Sarah got the message. All of a sudden she turned tail and fled. She did not know how long she had

been running but soon she was tired out. She stopped to look how far she had gone. There, right in front of her, was the road leading to her house. She ran up to the steps and knocked. "Come in." Sarah ran into her mother's arms. "What happened?" her mother enquired.

"Oh, mum, I just can't go back and face those terrible towers. They seem to stare at me out of two windows."

"Come on," her mother insisted. "I'll take you there."

Once again she went back to face those terrible towers but this time she was not afraid. When she reached the playground a tall man strode out to meet her. "Hello, Sarah," he said. "My name is Mr Davidson, I'm the head of this school."

Sarah took an instant liking to this man. "Sir," she enquired, "will I like this school?"

"Yes . . . I should think so," the head answered uncertainly.

Things went well for Sarah. The work was not too hard for her. In fact she was far ahead. She would sit reading a book, having finished ages ago. But a bad shock came when she had finished her work only to find that she had a headache. Although Mr Wheeler was strict he was not unkind. When he discovered her headache he investigated. On the decision that it was serious he sent her home. She was just leaving the gates when she felt a hand on her shoulder. She turned round. It was the head.

"What's up, Sarah?" he enquired.

"Oh, nothing. Just got a headache," said Sarah.

"Well, just come with me," suggested the head.

"Yes sir," agreed Sarah. But somehow her legs just wouldn't carry her. Then she fainted.

When she awoke she found herself in an odd room with all sorts of funny lights. She tried to struggle, but strangely she could not move. Then she tried to lift a finger but a peculiar fuzziness stopped her. She cried out for her mother. But there was no one, except lots of men with masks, buzzing about. She was extremely startled. Suddenly she was wheeled out on a trolley. She was relieved to see her mum. One man said, "Mrs Greenfield, your child had a serious attack of nerves. We suggest that she lives in the outback for a while."

"So that's why I came here," said my great-grandma, now wizened with age. She sighed as she looked out over the barren landscape. "And mind you, I don't feel like leaving." I laughed. "Now," she said, "your mum will be waiting for you." I glanced at the clock and heaved myself out of the armchair and put my coat on. How lucky I was to have a grandma like this! I opened the creaking gate and headed off in the direction of the Landrover.

Matthew Fenwick (9) Charlestown East PS

❧ I SURVIVED THE TITANIC ❧

I was born in 1900 and, with my family, lived in a small village in France. It was in 1912 that our family decided to move to the United States of America. In March that year we booked our passages on the "Titanic" to sail on its maiden voyage to New York. The date of its sailing was April the 10th, 1912. My sister was 14 years old when we boarded the liner and I was 12. We were saddened to be leaving France but we were excited to be on board the largest, fastest and most luxurious ship of its time. Also the ship was considered unsinkable. There were over 2000 people on board.

On Sunday, April 14th, after 4 days at sea, the weather turned bitterly cold. This forced many people to take shelter in their cabins. My sister and I had gone to our cabins early as we were feeling very cold. At about midnight we were awakened with a jolt. My sister screamed, "Something is WRONG!"

"Go back to sleep!" I said.

Soon one of the ship's crew came to our cabin and calmly told us to get up, put on our life jackets and make our way to the upper deck. Since we were second class passengers this meant that we had quite a long climb through several decks to reach the lifeboats. When we finally reached the upper deck a lifeboat was being loaded with women and children. Someone grabbed me from behind and pushed me into the lifeboat. I screamed for my sister who was frozen with fright. With the help of another passenger, who had just sadly farewelled his wife, they also pushed my sister into the lifeboat.

I was happy to be in the lifeboat but I was sad for those who were still on the sinking ship. As we rowed away we could still hear the band playing in the distance.

At 2.20 I saw her slide into the icy depths of the ocean. The sound of the screaming people still haunts me to this day.

Katrina Watkins (12) Leeton PS

❧ DISASTER ON THE RIVER ❧

It was 7.30 on a Sunday morning, and we were preparing to go on a camping holiday up to Darwin. All our family were going. There was myself, my sister and Mum and Dad. We loaded up the caravan and off we drove.

It was a long journey and after a week of stopping and sleeping in our caravan, we finally arrived in Darwin. We found a lovely caravan park. It was picturesque. The scenery was beautiful and it had a running river beside it. The trees were large oak trees which provided a lot of shade for the hot climate.

We toured around Darwin, which was fascinating, especially to see the newly built houses, because this was the city in 1974 that was devastated by cyclone Tracey. We arrived back at our caravan park that night feeling tired, and fell asleep straight away.

We woke up bright and early the next morning. It was going to be an exciting day, as we were going fishing. Where we were going to fish we had to be careful, because, even though it was a good fishing spot, it was near a crocodile infested area.

After breakfast, we all set off to the river. We arrived at the river and we hired a boat for the day. Dad put all our worms on the hooks because worms are so squishy that we didn't want to touch them. We threw our lines in. We sat in our boat for a while before we even got a nibble, and in the distance we could see the crocodiles floating around in the water; they just looked like big wooden logs.

During the day we noticed some very adventurous fishermen, fishing on the banks of the river, and some were even wading in a bit.

I suddenly got a nibble on the line. Golly, it was exciting. I said, "Mummy, come and have a look at what I caught" — and she came.

"How smashing my dear, oh we shall have a feast tonight." Dad thought it was wonderful too.

The men on the shore seemed to be wading out further and further.

Dad was getting worried, mainly because the crocodiles were coming nearer and nearer. The men didn't seem to notice this.

Dad yelled out to the men to get out of the water, but they were too far away to hear.

The crocodiles seemed to be coming faster now and Dad started waving his arms about and yelling.

One particular crocodile was moving very silently and swiftly and suddenly was very close to the man.

The man suddenly turned around and saw the crocodile. He started swimming quickly to the banks. But he just wasn't quick enough, and the crocodile grabbed hold of his foot and started flicking backwards and forwards.

How horrifying it was to watch! I quickly turned my head away. Another fisherman quickly rushed to his aid. But he couldn't do much good because the crocodile was thrashing this man about furiously. As the crocodile was turning to pull the man in, he opened his mouth to get a better grip, and the man scrambled ashore. The fishermen around him pulled him high up on the bank. The wounds to his leg were horrific. Half his foot was missing and his leg was ripped to shreds.

The men rushed to get help, and we came into shore. Dad jumped out to see if there was anything he could do.

The man was still conscious, but in very bad pain. The ambulance came and took him away.

We pulled our boat out of the water and we all went back to the caravan park feeling very shaken and sorry for the man who was half eaten, realising it is very dangerous to fish in a crocodile infested area. We didn't go back to that fishing area again, although we did fish once more elsewhere.

For the rest of the holiday, we saw many sights in Darwin, and after two weeks we packed up to start our long journey home. But before we went, we went to the hospital to see how the man was feeling. He was feeling a lot better; although he was still in a lot of pain.

It took us another week to arrive home. What an exciting holiday we had!!

Kara Richardson (11) Sturt PS, Wagga Wagga

JUST SITTING AND THINKING

We had moved into a new house about a month before. I was still going to my other school. I just took two buses. I liked living in our new house. It was near the beach, and it was a two storied house. Our other one wasn't. I still went to baseball practice with Betty. I met her there every Saturday.

But then it all changed.

It was seven o'clock on a summer evening. I ran down the beach, still white with anger. A big wave splashed on me so I took my clothes off. I had my costume on and I had brought down a towel with me. I was alone on the beach. Nobody was to be seen.

Yesterday I had been dropped from the baseball team!

After five years with my friends, scoring points, getting people out and playing my best, I was dropped from the team because a stupid new girl came. I can't even remember her name and I'm glad I can't. They decided to throw me out just because I lived the furthest away, and the team couldn't care less. They forgot all about me, even including Betty.

"Ah, go for a swim, forget about them," said a little voice in my mind.

It was very late. Even the surfies had gone but I couldn't care less. I dived under a wave and I felt my body come alive in the cold. I swam powerfully towards the setting sun for a few minutes and then turned to face the beach. I was drawing away from the beach every second. I tried to reach the bottom with my foot, and found nothing. I gasped.

I swam easily towards the shore. I was still annoyed. After a while I decided I had swum enough and I reached for the bottom. Again I couldn't feel the sand. I dipped my head under the water and saw dark currents around my feet, as if the sea was deeper. I raised my head and looked for the beach. I was still far away from home. I felt cold and scared. It was getting darker and darker. I felt stranded — alone in the water.

"All right Eva, you'll have to fight for it. Don't be scared. You're not afraid are you?" I asked myself.

"I sure am," I said aloud. Nothing but the rip I was caught in heard me. I was a long way from home now.

"Stop that, all you have to do is cross the rip. Forget about the beach for a while," I said to myself again.

I saw a rock cliff that made the beach look like a bay. I concentrated on a large rock, fixing my eyes on it. Every stroke I took, it simply slid sideways towards the beach. I was still in the rip. I forced myself to go faster but I flooded my throat through my open mouth. I was exhausted. I could even feel the weight of my muscles. I became helpless. There was that little message on the inside of my mind. It was saying, "You are not going to get out. The rip is too fast, it won't let you climb out, you are going to drown."

"Stop it!" I shouted. I wasn't going to stay in the middle of the sea all night and drown myself. Maybe there is someone on the beach — someone I didn't see, I thought. I waved my arm and shouted. It sounded like a tired seagull. It was no use. I gave up.

What now? I thought. All I have to do now is get swept out until the rip stops. It will stop, but it will be cold and dark then. I might even be two or three kilometres out. I can't swim that far. Yee! I'll end up in the ocean and, of course, there are sharks.

"Stop!" I said again aloud. I shouldn't think like that. I started fighting the sea as though it was human. I was about to open my mouth and scream, but No! I thought. That will do no good. I'll just lose my breath.

I was stroking for the shore again. I said to myself, "Just swim fast, faster than the rip, so fast that you cannot think."

The water was pushing me now and it was making it easier for me to swim, but the hard thing about it was that I couldn't see a thing. I only felt my weight and my aching body.

Eventually I felt a pain on my side increasing with every kick. "You can't go on," the voice said. I accidentally swallowed water. I coughed and swam heavily on. Seaweed caught my right leg but I ignored it. I swam on.

The fingers of my left hand felt something. My eyes stared hard in the black water and my brain tried to understand what was happening. My right hand scooped sand and, in a moment, an angry wave tumbled me onto the beach.

It took half an hour before I was able to pull myself to my feet. I walked back to my towel, picked it up and wrapped it around me and walked slowly towards my house. I was still exhausted. My throat ached, my body ached, everything ached.

For a while I could not remember why I had gone for a swim, tired and in dangerous and deserted water at sunset. When I remembered I found it hard to believe.

I could see my house by now. Thank God there weren't any police cars outside my house.

There's a tree just outside my room. I climbed it and climbed through the window and jumped into my room. I reached the light and switched it on.

"Phew, that was close," I said to myself. I got some clean clothes and had a shower. When I had finished I opened the door and sneaked quickly down to the laundry to put my dirty clothes into the washing basket. As I quietly ran back upstairs to my room I bumped into my Dad.

"And where were you Miss?" he asked me.

I answered, "Down at the beach."

"I hope you weren't swimming."

"Oh no," I said, "I was just sitting and thinking."

Eva Karagiannis (11) Concord West PS

"What page is it on? It should have made the front page, who do they think they are? Ah! here it is on page 3. It didn't get much coverage on the box . . . Damn! wish my hands would stop trembling."

A police spokesman has issued a statement on the vicious killing of 21 year old Nancy Corbet who was found today murdered. The girl's throat was cut after she had been bound and tortured in the lounge room of her inner city apartment. Police cannot identify a motive for this gruesome slaying but say they are following up several leads. They commented on the striking similarity between this killing and the several killings in the new box office hit "Changes in Reality" which was released in the city theatres last week. Police suspect the murderer may have been influenced by the film. If this is true police psychologists warn that there may be further killings as the person responsible for this murder may be mentally unstable.

Mum was right, I can't do anything properly. I haven't even made the front page of the Sun. She always said I was a failure and I'd never amount to anyone. Just because I used to spend all my time with books and at the theatre and preferred to go to NIDA instead of doing Science or Medicine . . . She reckoned I was weird. She never forgave me when dad left home . . . She used to give him a hell of a time because he never made it to a white collar worker. You're just like your father a nothing! . . It wasn't my fault . . . I don't blame him for decking her!! I don't blame him for clearing out, but God it left me in the "front line".

That was the great thing about acting, I could escape from her. Every day I could change my reality by becoming someone else — not Markus the nobody, but Markus the lover, the tycoon, the soldier, the detective, or even the psychopath. That was a great role. I really loved the part of the psychopath in "Changes in Reality" each time I killed one of those women. I felt like I was getting my own back on my mother. Failure! . . . Failure! . . . Failure! . . . I'll show you, you rotten old cow, this time I'll make the front page of every damn newspaper in the country, you'll have enough headlines to paper your whole house. If star billing isn't enough for you, I'll give you nation-wide headlines.

"Oh! it's you, come in Markus, what's wrong? You look strange . . . What is it? Markus stop it, what are you doing, Markus stop . . . stop."

"Hello mother, I've just come to visit you, I've come to show you just how I'm going to be successful. Stop struggling mother, it will be easier to breathe with the plaster over your mouth if you stop struggling. We'll just have to tighten these wrist bands mother . . . we can't have you running away now, can we? You'll miss the show mother. After all you're the star of the show mother. It's nice of you to help me be successful mother, we can be successful together now. Do you like my friend mother? His edge is so sharp you won't feel him as he caresses your throat."

"Members of the jury how do you find the accused?"
"Guilty my Lord."

Catharine Pruscino (10) Balmain PS

❧ THE POWER OF LOVE ❧

Our car veered towards the centre of the road, crashing through the fence and off the embankment. Everything went black . . . .

I opened my eyes and found myself staring at a white ceiling. With horror I realised that I was in hospital. Then suddenly, the terror of the night before all came back to me. The party, and the lift home with my friends. Eric, the driver, was drunk and I knew it, but I didn't want to be the party pooper by saying he shouldn't drive. After that I couldn't remember anything.

I looked around at the room I was in. There was a doctor and 3 nurses looking over me exchanging worried glances. My mother was sitting on my bed. I opened my mouth to say something but nothing came out. I tried to lift my arm, but it stayed still, unmoving and lifeless. There was something wrong, terribly wrong. I heard bits of the hospital staff's conversation, they were using words like "coma" and "brain-damage". A sudden wave of tiredness crept over me and I closed my eyes to sleep.

When I woke my mother was the only one in the room. She was sitting on my bed, slowly massaging my lifeless limbs. When she saw me open my eyes her face lit up with hope, but fell again when I showed no response.

"Hello darling," she whispered softly, "how are you feeling?" A tear began to roll down her cheek. I wanted to reach out and hold her and say I was all right, but my limbs would not respond to my brain's commands. I was now feeling frightened and confused. What was wrong with me? How come I could hear and understand everyone around me, but they couldn't understand me? Questions jumbled around in my frustrated brain. My mother called in a nurse who began stroking my hair. From bits of their conversation I learnt that I had been asleep for days. Suddenly the gentle stroking became vigorous rubbing. The nurse put cold ice packs against my cheeks and started moving my arms. It was agony. What were they trying to do, I wondered. Couldn't they see I was awake? Gradually the exercising stopped and I fell asleep again.

For days the gruelling procedures continued. Each day there were new and different exercises. They blew whistles, rubbed my limbs and scrubbed my feet with a rough scrubbing brush. But nothing helped, my body was still and unmoving. My speech was just the same. The only thing I could do was swallow soft food. I had been in hospital for what seemed an eternity when my mother told me that the hospital had said I could go home. I was thrilled but I only wished I could have thanked all the doctors and nurses for trying to help me.

At home my progress was the same. I slept most of the time. But one morning everything changed.

I awoke as the sun was filtering across my bedroom. Mum, as usual, was sitting by the bed. When she saw me open my eyes she held my hand.

"Good morning sweetheart," she whispered and squeezed my hand. Again I concentrated on squeezing her hand back. Slowly, bit by bit, for the first time in months my hand closed on my mother's. Tears rolled down her cheeks and slowly I said my first words.

"I love you."

Bronwyn Adcock (11) Milton PS

LONGER STORIES

❧ THE MYSTERY OF THE MONSTER IN ❧ HALLBAS LAKE

1 This is the story about two cubs and two brownies named Mark, Darran, Kate and Sarah. They were very nice children. They were loving and caring but very adventurous.

Mrs Baigly was a very nice woman but very clever too. She was the live-in housekeeper of the Vanie family. Just now she was packing a bottle of lemonade, eight ham sandwiches and a couple of bars of chocolate for the children's picnic by Hallbas Lake.

They decided to take the long way to the lake because it was such a sunny Sunday afternoon. They saw all the rabbits popping out of their holes and rushing in again very rapidly. They saw the lizards running out through the cracks, the ants working and the birds twittering.

2 Soon they came to Hallbas Lake. The boys lay down while the girls unpacked their lunches. Everybody sat down on the grassy bank and enjoyed their sandwiches. They had walked a long way so they were grateful to have a cool drink of lemonade.

Suddenly Kate (who was very observant) shouted, "Look over there." She pointed in the direction where the ducks, who had been peacefully swimming, had fluttered away and there was a pool of bubbles in the centre. They all looked and they all saw a hump rising slowly out of the water. A moment later there was an ear-splitting crash, an enormous muddy wave. It was gone.

The girls had screamed. The boys, though very frightened, had watched intensely. When the girls thought that it had gone, which was about five minutes later, they looked up from their laps. They were still very frightened.

When Kate and Sarah had recovered they asked the boys what had happened. "Well," Mark began, "you saw the hump rising up."

"Yes we did," replied the girls.

"Then came the splash and up came a small dinosaur-like head. It opened its mouth and boy, you should have seen its teeth!"

"Wow!" Sarah exclaimed. "The Loch Ness has Nessie, Loon Lake has Loonie so why not Bassie for Hallbas Lake?"

Now these children could have seen something wonderful but unfortunately they didn't.

By evening almost all the neighbourhood knew about their find. The children were interviewed by the newspaper and television reporters. By now they were very happy little kids.

3   The next day they were being questioned by their friends in the village playground when a ten year old girl named Tinkerbell came along. She was dressed in very grand clothes. Almost everyone knew her because she was the daughter of a very rich man who lived in a great mansion.

She said sharply, "Darran Vanie, I don't believe you saw that 'Monster' yesterday. I've been out all morning, sitting on that muddy bank, getting my dress dirty, looking for it."

Poor Darran wasn't put off easily. He knew that he had seen Bassie with his own eyes. He felt like fighting Tinkerbell but he knew he couldn't.

The next day they decided to go down to Hallbas Lake again. This time the monster stayed up for fifteen seconds. Mark got a pretty good photograph of it. Now no-one could say it didn't exist.

The next day they showed the beautiful colour photo of what seemed to be the monster, to their friends. Angus Polly-wopple studied the photograph carefully. Then he exclaimed, "What is this then?" He pointed to where nails and screws joined metal! Darran, Mark, Kate and Sarah were flabber-gasted! They stood still gazing into space while Angus smiled and smiled. Angus was right!

4   The next thing they had to do was find the faker, so early next morning they set off for Hallbas Lake once again. They took a picnic lunch again and they saw the monster again.

This time the children waited after they had seen Bassie. They hid and waited to see what would happen. They saw the "monster" come out of the water and a man get out. Sarah scribbled down his details on her notepad. This is what she wrote: brown hair, beard, Ghostbusters T-shirt, blue jeans, glasses, black bag.

5   The children called him Mr X. They didn't want to tell the police. They told somebody though. They told it to Mrs Whinny the Witch. Mrs Witch lived in 1 Wintelthorp Way, Wumbly. She was a good witch and the children's friend.

When they told her the whole story, from beginning to end, she was very interested. After a while she croaked (she had a very bad cold), "I have a plan. All you have to do is not go down to the lake for a couple of weeks and I'll do the rest."

The two weeks passed quickly. Kate went to Whinny's house but she wasn't there. "She must have a plan in action," she thought and Kate was right.

In fact, right then, Mrs Witch had just put her plan in action.

Poor Mr X had got tired of the children not going there so he decided that he would act the monster all the same. The witch, meanwhile, was on her broomstick watching everything from the heavens. She was expecting this to happen.

After about half an hour Mr X grew tired of monster faking and anyway, he wanted his dinner. As soon as he stepped out of his contraption, Whinny zoomed down on her broomstick, collected an astounded Mr X and zoomed back up towards the sun and clouds.

When she had landed safely on a cloud she said severely to Mr X, "Why in the world are you puzzling and frightening the people of the village? You ought to be ashamed of yourself."

Well, Mr X was lost for words.

"How did you know I was faking?" sulked Mr X.

"You have not answered my question," yelled Whinny.

"Oh, alright," complained Mr X, "I just wanted to have some fun."

"Fun indeed, just you wait," screamed Whinny. She was in a real rage. "And what is your name, may I ask?" raged Whinny.

"W-W-W-Well," stammered Mr X, "it . . is . . actually Randolph Rickywood."

"What comedian would have a name like that?" shouted the witch. "I'm going to jail you on the moon for two years."

Well, that was the end of that. Everyone lived happily ever after, except Randolph Rickywood that is, because the mystery had been solved!

Till, tail, tout,
My tale's told out!

Zehra Koroglu (8) Putney PS

From UFO

1. The Disappearance

It was Thursday, 27th July. When the bell rang at 9.25 a.m. at Kooringal Primary School everyone went to their classroom, as usual. They gathered their books and went to Maths. When Maths was over they returned to their own rooms and worked until the bell rang for recess.

3 Red put their books under their desks. They went out to the hat room and took their food from their bags. Mrs D. was still in Room 12. Everyone ran into the playground. To their surprise they didn't see or hear anyone.

For a few minutes nobody worried because they thought that they were out early. When Suzie looked at her watch, it was 11.10 a.m. — and they were still the only ones in the playground. She told the rest of 3 Red that recess was nearly over and there was still no-one around. It seemed really peculiar. They all decided to search the school to find out where everyone was. They agreed to meet again in ten minutes.

2. Multicoloured Lights

Ten minutes later they all met outside the canteen. The school was bare, except for 3 Red. So they decided to return to Room 12 and tell Mrs D. At first she didn't believe them . . . . . . until 3 Red took her out and showed her. She believed them then!

She ran up to the office and nervously phoned the Department of Education and the police to report the missing people. Naturally, nobody really believed her but they said they would come out, just to keep her quiet. I mean to say, whoever heard of a whole school disappearing?

While they were waiting for help to come, they decided to investigate the mystery themselves. Katie, who didn't need glasses (like Mrs D.) happened to look out the window and up at the sky. "Gosh!" she said. "Have a look at that thing!"

She pointed towards a multicoloured light travelling in a swooping manner across the sky . . .

from an eight-chapter story by a Year 3 Group (8) Kooringal PS

❧ From A PURPLE MYSTERY ❧

(This long and ingeniously structured story blends dream and actuality. The following episode centres on the dream version of what Joel and Ciryn Williams had actually done the night before.)

. . . Just as Joel walked into the kitchen the front door opened. Joel went to see who it was. A very tall, well built man walked in. He wore purple gloves and a matching purple coloured suit. Joel felt there was something strange about the man.

"That's the man," Ciryn gasped, trying not to show her scaredness. "It's the purple man. The one that I saw out the window last night when we were — "

"SShh!" Joel interrupted. "She's just a bit scared this morning for some reason," he explained to Mr and Mrs Williams who were looking confused.

"Hold on," Mr Williams started. "Where were you last night? And what were you doing?"

"Nothing daddy." Ciryn started to cry. "I didn't do it, honest daddy. Joel made me do it. He told me to. It's all his fault." Ciryn turned to Joel. "I told you we would get into trouble. I hate you, Joel." Ciryn reached up on the shelf for a tissue to blow her nose and wipe her eyes.

"Don't talk nonsense," Mrs Williams said feeling a bit weak still. "And what's this about Joel making you do it? What did you do?"

"Well, you see-um-ah-well — " Joel didn't know how to tell his parents.

"Come on Joel, tell us what you did," Mr Williams asked. "You can tell us what you were doing and then Ciryn can tell us who or what she saw. Agree?"

"Yes, O.K." Joel said. "Well we wanted to know what the surprise was so Ciryn and I got out of bed when you and mum went to bed, we went into the kitchen to see what the surprise was." Joel then started mumbling. "I got a torch and Ciryn and I looked at the games — "

"Joel," exclaimed Mrs Williams, "I don't understand a word you said. Would you please stop mumbling so we might be able to understand what you are trying to say."

"Yes mum," Joel said.

"Thank you," said Mrs Williams. "Continue from where you got a torch or something."

"O.K." Joel thought over what he was going to say for a couple of seconds. Then he began. "I got the torch from the cupboard." This time Joel was talking much clearer than before. "Ciryn and I looked at the games. When we were looking at them Ciryn went white and — "

"Hold on," Mr Williams interrupted. "You mean you, you and Ciryn, got up at about midnight?"

"Yes dad," said Joel expecting Mr Williams to blow a fuse or something, but to Joel's surprise he didn't get mad at all. He just asked Ciryn to tell him why she went white.

"I didn't go white daddy." Ciryn was against what Joel said in a way. "I did get scared stiff though, but I didn't go white," she protested. Mr Williams just told her to go on with it, so she did. "What made me go white, I mean what made me scared," Ciryn corrected herself hastily, "was a purple thing. It looked like that man. It did daddy, honestly." Ciryn pointed to the tall, well built man dressed in purple.

"Ciryn, please don't point, it's very rude honey," Mrs Williams said eyeing Ciryn in a disappointed way.

"Why didn't you tell us what happened before?" asked Mr

Williams. "Anyway is that all?"

"No," Ciryn said to him. "Then —"

"Hey, I was telling it," interrupted Joel. "Then I told her not to be stupid because there is no such thing as a purple person. Anyway, then there was this huge purple light that filled the room."

"That's when me and Joel ran back to bed, we were scared," added Ciryn.

"And then when we went to bed, I thought that I'd better tidy up the mess. See, we didn't pack up the games. I was heading towards the kitchen when I heard a person's footsteps, I ran straight back to bed."

"Is that all?" asked the man in the purple suit. He had been taking down everything that Joel had been saying. Joel nodded his head. Ciryn ran to her room, she was certain that the man was the same man as she had seen out the window last night. Joel, listening to the man in the purple suit walk back and forth in the kitchen, knew that he had heard the same footsteps that night in the kitchen, they had the same rhythm . . .

Yvette Covassin (11) OLQP Greystanes

❧ CHAPTER ONE: KIDNAPPED ❧

The soft whisper in the willows echoed in the ridges above. A dust storm was brewing in the west. Children were playing in the quiet river. The eldest boy looked to be twelve. He was poking fun at a girl a year younger.

"Elucidate," the boy demanded.

She whirled on him and he pretended to cringe with fright.

"I take 'elucidate' back," he howled. "I take it all back. What I meant was explain, make clear your statement, Miss Steiyn."

The girl giggled. "I can't explain, make clear or elucidate. I just feel it in my bones."

He groaned. "Feminine intuition. Gleeps noodlehead, spare us that."

"I'll spare you that and a lot more," the girl said tartly. "I was just going to explain, make clear and elucidate to you about the reason we haven't had any rain yet! But, since I'm a noodlehead, I'd better keep it to myself."

"I modify that statement," the boy said promptly. "You're not a noodlehead, you're merely equipped with scrambled brains."

"Brad, Jo," their mother called. "Mr Labottomy wants his dinner, and you know I haven't the courage to feed him."

Jo grinned as she swung herself up onto the verandah.

"And you also know he won't hurt you," she replied slyly.

The four children at Andarra cattle station, Brad, 13, the eldest; Jo, 12; Michael and Bronia, both 11, seldom saw their father. He was often away mustering, and his wife was left to hold the fort. But this was one time that he was at home.

Brad pushed the door to Mr Labottomy's room open. He was an anaconda. As soon as they entered the room, the anaconda began rubbing itself against the cage bars, a signal that it wanted food.

"O.K., mate, out you come." He lifted Mr Labottomy gently, and the snake curled around his neck lovingly.

Major, the cockatoo, squawked impatiently from his perch on the chandelier. Jo walked over to his feed bin and tipped some in. Major flew over to it in delight.

The door opened a crack, and a blue and white budgie flew into the room.

"Hello, Bluey," Brad called to the twittering heap of feathers. The door opened wider and Michael walked in. Glenn was at his heels. The border collie barked with joy as he sighted his friends.

Brad and Jo yelled together, "No, boy, Glenn no. Down boy!" But it was too late. Their dog, his tail streaming behind him like a banner, flung himself briefly at Brad's chest. Then he turned and launched himself into one, final, joyful leap.

He caught Jo off balance, and pinned her to the floor with one great paw, and then smothered her face with kisses. It took the combined efforts of Brad and Michael to pull him off.

At dinner that night, their father announced that their prize jersey was pregnant. It would mean extra money, so they could start ploughing the back paddock.

The children, Major, Mr Labottomy, Bluey and Glenn wandered down to the river. When they got back, an hour later, the house was in an uproar.

One of the stablehands explained: "I was grooming the master's horse when I heard loud screams. I raced to the house, only to find no one. They took the horses. I'm afraid they've been kidnapped.". . .

from an eleven-chapter story by Julie Horan (11) Old Guildford PS

From FARMER SMITZ

"Dat der foxes has been at my quackers and squawkers," Farmer Smitz growled angrily. He strode quickly down the frost-bitten path. The frost nipped at his cold fingers. He was angry. He could tell that the foxes had been into his poultry. There were feathers here and feathers there. They stuck in the wire netting. They were all through the ponds.

"One of deese here days I'll pepper their tails," he mumbled crossly. He stamped over to where the fox had dug in.

"You'd fink dem foxey loxey would have his dinner at one of my ducks but no, he has many, many."

Slowly Farmer Smitz walked round the rest of the farm. He was dismayed to see the foxes had got into his lovely prize show ducks.

"Damn, damn 'em," Farmer Smitz mumbled to himself.

Later that morning as Farmer Smitz was checking through the incubators he found twenty five per cent of his duck eggs had not hatched when they were supposed to. Further testing showed they were rotten, or malformed.

After his lunch he went into town to sell his poultry. He dawdled out to his old Ford ute. The ute had been blue when it was new but now it was a bluish white and riddled with rust spots. It had dints in its lining. The tail gate groaned, like a dungeon door opening. The interior was just as bad as the exterior. None of the gadgets on the dashboard worked. When the engine started it sounded like an aeroplane conking out. In all it was a rust bucket. Even the most understanding people in the town made jokes about it. But Farmer Smitz could not see these obvious faults. It was one of his pride and joys.

He laughed to himself as the engine got to a choking start. The old rust bucket bungled and rattled into town. Tangalong, the town, was reasonably big. Farmer Smitz parked where he always parked. He took his birds to the main street where he usually sold them. Business was worse that day than it had been for a long while. No one bought any of his birds. The only person he saw was Mrs Oakley, the Delicatessen owner. She was a fat woman. She had brown curly hair, fat chubby cheeks and she almost always wore an apron. Today she was wearing a big woollen jumper with sheep on the front. Farmer Smitz saw the big lady coming. He pretended not to see her.

"Hello," she boomed in her loudest voice.

"Hello," replied Farmer Smitz.

"Um, I'm going to have to cancel my order for the poultry," she said quickly and rushed off.

Farmer Smitz packed up his birds and drove out of town. On his way home he crossed a low bridge. He stopped, got out and sat down. He thought for a long while. He seemed at peace with bubbling, swirling waters that trickled and bubbled under his feet. Farmer Smitz was just about to depart when he saw a hessian bag floating down the river. The bag jiggled and a faint whimpering came from it. Farmer Smitz knew the cruel way that people disposed of unwanted pups or kittens. Farmer Smitz glanced around and saw a long stick. He picked it up and reached.

"Drat, too short," he growled, disappointed. Farmer Smitz hurried to the back of his ute. He searched around and finally found a piece of wire. Farmer Smitz ran down the bank and caught up with the bag. Farmer Smitz reached out, holding the hook . . . . . just hooked it.

"Phew, dat was clouse," Farmer Smitz puffed.

A small whining came from the bag.

"Now dwot do we have here," he snorted as he opened the bag. "Ah, a little puppy," he laughed, "but you're all full of water. We'll fix dat."

He picked the small, fragile pup up in his big hands and pressed firmly on his lungs. The pup coughed and spluttered.

"We'll soon have you home," whispered Farmer Smitz, as he picked up the limp pup and took him to the dilapidated ute.

When he got home he put the pup in front of the heater inside a crate with a pillow inside. In the morning Farmer Smitz almost forgot about the little pup. It was after breakfast that he remembered him. He tiptoed over to the crate and peered inside. Instead of a sick little pup he saw nothing. Then he heard growling and felt a tugging at his trouser leg.

"I fink we better call you Teaser." He grinned at the name. "Yes, I think that is a good name."

Teaser stopped growling and pulling at Farmer Smitz' trouser leg and looked up at his owner with a lop-sided grin.

"Come on," Farmer Smitz laughed as he picked up the pup in his big hands. Teaser bit a hold of his leather hands. The pup's pin-like teeth left little holes to add to the collection of scars.

"Dar, don't do that," he ordered with a frown. Then his frown relaxed into a grin and he was soon playing with the pup.

Farmer Smitz walked down to his poultry shed. Teaser followed, trying to bite Farmer Smitz' feet. Farmer Smitz examined his poultry. He found that something, most probably a fox, had chewed through some of the wire but to Farmer Smitz' relief the fox had not succeeded in getting through. Suddenly there was a growl, a bark and hissing all at once. Then a frightened yelp and a howl. Then Teaser came tearing round the corner, his tail underneath his legs as though it had been stuck to his belly. There, in pursuit, were three ganders, hissing, squawking, slapping and waddling as fast as they could go. Teaser ran straight to Farmer Smitz. The geese, seeing Farmer Smitz, retreated. Teaser gave them a warning growl from the safety of his master's legs . . .

(Teaser soon learns to live with the poultry, and a year or so later, fully grown, he pursues and kills a fox after Farmer Smitz' ducks. The story ends thus.)

The moon came out from behind a cloud and flooded the night life with its light. Teaser limped towards his home. He stopped at times to lick his wounds. Teaser made it to the incubation shed and there in the warmth he lay sprawled out. When he awoke he was in a basket in front of a fire with stitches in his cuts and bandages on most parts of his body.

He glanced up and saw a man with a vet's bag. He looked to where his master sat. There he was, with a faint grin on his face. His usually colourful cheeks were paled. His large hands lay in his lap. His big belly hung out like a bean bag and he was wearing his brown leather sandals.

"That fox fights like hell but you fight like two hells."

Charles Cay (12) Lowesdale PS